How and Why Stories
for Readers Theatre

How and Why Stories
for Readers Theatre

Judy Wolfman

Teacher Ideas Press
Portsmouth, NH

Teacher Ideas Press
A division of Reed Elsevier Inc.
361 Hanover Street
Portsmouth, NH 03801-3912
www.teacherideaspress.com

Offices and agents throughout the world

Library of Congress Cataloging-in-Publication Data

Wolfman, Judy.
    How and why stories for readers theatre / Judy Wolfman.
        p. cm.
    Includes index.
    ISBN 1-59469-006-5 (alk. paper)
    1. Children's plays, American. 2. Drama in education—Problems, exercises, etc. 3. Readers' theater—Study and teaching (Elementary) I. Title.
    PS3623.O585H69 2004
    812'.6—dc22   2004004373

Editor: Suzanne Barchers
Production Coordinator: Angela Laughlin
Typesetter: Westchester Book Services
Cover design: Gaile Ivaska
Manufacturing: Steve Bernier

Printed in the United States of America on acid-free paper

08 07 06 05 04 ML 1 2 3 4 5

To Tony Fredericks, my mentor and friend.
Thank you for your faith, encouragement, and inspiration.
To Suzanne Barchers, my editor, who guided me and
patiently answered my many questions.

Contents

Birds

Insects

Plants and Trees

Reptiles

Contents

Sea and Sky

Preface

Ever since I can remember, I've always enjoyed acting. Nothing made me happier than becoming someone else. Often I created plays in which I could develop a character, and it wasn't unusual to hear me assume several characters using a variety of voices and expressions.

One summer, I convinced several of my friends to be in my plays, promising that they wouldn't have to memorize their lines—just read them with expression. Little did I know that as a twelve-year-old kid, I was doing my first readers theatre.

After practicing several scripts, my group decided to perform for our parents, friends, and neighbors. My front yard was the stage area, and the audience sat on the screened-in front porch of my house. We were a success! The parents encouraged us to put on more shows throughout the summer.

When school began in the fall, my readers theatre experiences came to an abrupt halt. It wasn't until several years later, when I taught first grade, that it re-entered my life.

I was delighted that my first graders had mastered their vocabulary words and were able to use their phonetic skills to attack new words. But their reading was flat, with no expression. After praising the readers for knowing their words, I often asked them to read it again "with expression." That didn't work, and the students and I became frustrated.

In desperation, I tried to think of new ways to help them read with expression, and then it hit me: readers theatre! I developed several scripts based on my students' favorite books and stories, made enough copies for each class member, and proceeded to "act" while reading. It worked! I don't know who was more pleased, my students or me.

Readers theatre became the popular way to read in my classroom from that day on. Initially the students would ask if we could "act and read," but soon they learned to call it by what it was—readers theatre.

As a teacher, I was delighted with their expressive reading, their cooperative efforts, and the way their self-esteem escalated. They were proud of themselves, and so confident of their skills that they requested doing a program for their parents, other classes, the principal, and anyone else they wanted to invite.

Our scripts grew and went beyond classroom material. Because my students frequently asked me "how" and "why" questions (Why is the sky blue? How do seeds grow into flowers?), I became interested in *pourquoi* stories. *Pourquoi* (por-kwa) is a French word that means "why," and it usually explains why things in nature are the way they are.

I wrote this book of scripts based on pourquoi stories that stem from folktales of many countries as well as Native American Indian legends that attempt to give the answers to "how" and "why" questions with imaginative and creative stories. It was interesting to get to know the various stories from different origins, and compare their similarities and differences. These scripts are my adaptations in which I have given the characters names, added descriptions and dialogue, and in some cases, created additional characters. However, I have not altered the main storylines of the original folktales and legends.

As you use these scripts with your students, all of you should enjoy the explanations of how and why things are. Readers theatre will allow your readers to become new characters, and to enjoy the thrill that the combination of reading and acting provides. So, prepare yourself for fun!

Judy Wolfman

Introduction

What Is Readers Theatre?

Readers Theatre introduces children to a story by using a script as the format for reading aloud. It is creative oral reading of any form of literature, on any grade level. Through effective oral interpretation, characters express their thoughts and feelings, and with readers and a good script, a story comes to life. Readers theatre is an exciting cross between reading and dramatics—and children love it!

Readers theatre isn't limited to the classroom. It is an effective activity for religious school classes, libraries, theatres, clubs and organizations, neighborhood get-togethers, and family enjoyment. Here, however, our focus is on the classroom.

Why Use Readers Theatre?

Because the emphasis of readers theatre is on reading, the obvious value is to assist readers of all ages and levels in interpreting literature, reading smoothly and with expression, and enjoying reading in a nonthreatening environment. However, readers theatre goes beyond just reading. Other values of readers theatre include the following:

1. It allows several children to participate at the same time, each child gets an opportunity to have a turn, and each child can present his or her unique interpretation of the same role. There is no right or wrong interpretation.

2. Non-English speaking students and reluctant readers see and hear the language in action, and use previous readers as role models. Many scripts have easy reader, repetitive, or group lines that can get them started. These students recognize that readers theatre isn't scary, and they are more willing to try a solo part.

3. As readers theatre is used in the classroom, oral language, vocabulary, and communication skills strengthen. Students project their voices, articulate better, and use their voices expressively, with intonation and inflection. These skills will be carried over into other aspects of public speaking in the future.

4. Because students interact with each other while using readers theatre, it supports teamwork and cooperation. It is not a competitive but a cooperative activity in which students listen attentively to each other, share their thoughts about the story and its characters, and help each other with interpretations.

5. As students work through a scripted story, their imaginations get to work and they create visual images of the characters and settings. In addition, critical thinking and comprehension are enhanced as students study and analyze the elements of the story: plot, theme, setting, point of view, and characterization.

6. Through the group's support system, students develop self-confidence and self-esteem, enabling them to become stronger readers, while bringing the story to life.

7. Readers theatre helps children appreciate a well-written story and various forms of literature, and it stimulates enthusiasm and a love for reading.

8. In readers theatre, stories are repeated using different readers, thus reinforcing the story or concept without redundancy or boredom.

9. Readers theatre is easy to use, requiring no memorization, costumes, sets, props, blocking, or elaborate staging, unless desired.

10. Finally, and perhaps best of all, readers theatre is informal, relaxing, and fun! It is non-threatening and not scary for the student, and it requires no special drama training on the part of the teacher. Love for a good story, the ability to read, a good script, and a willingness to try readers theatre will make it happen in your classroom.

How to Use Readers Theatre

There are accepted practices for readers theatre, however it can be adapted. Teachers will discover what works best, but here are a few suggestions to serve as a guide.

Get Ready (Plan and Prepare)

1. Script Preparation—Choose a script and evaluate it in terms of content, reading level (RL), vocabulary, and presentation possibilities. Make enough copies of the script so that each member of the class will have one. Make one or two extras in case you need to replace any. Place each script in its own folder or binder to help preserve it. The title of the script can be printed on the cover for ease in finding it for future readings. You may want to highlight each character's name in one complete set, using a different color for each one. This master set is helpful to the teacher for following the reading. In each individual script, the character's name should be highlighted throughout. This helps the reader stay on track.

2. Understanding Readers Theatre—Bring the children together and sit with them in a circle. The first time you use readers theatre, explain that this is a fun way to read using expression. Emphasize that they will not have to memorize anything, but they will interpret their parts and read them effectively. Tell them that they will all have a chance to read.

3. Preparing to Read—To help the children understand what is meant by expressiveness, you may want to do some warm-ups and vocal activities. (a) Breathing. Take shallow breaths while talking (any phrase will do). Then take deep breaths and talk as the air is expelled. With deep breathing, words should be louder and more distinct. (b) Mouth warm-ups. Stretch the mouth from side to side, and up and down. Wiggle the tongue in all directions. This makes the mouth and tongue more flexible. While doing the exercises, make sounds, too. (c) Using individual vowels and consonants, say each one quietly at first, getting louder and louder, but not screaming! (d) Take a single word (oh, ah) and say it as a question, as though the light bulb just went on. Say it with disappointment, with surprise, with sadness, and so forth. Use different volume levels as well. So many ways to express one word! Pick your own words to use. (e) Use a word and say it while changing volume levels, pitch, and pace (fast or slow). Try various inflections and intonations. Experiment! (f) Do the same exercise, only this time use a complete phrase. For example, *I am so mad. Can't you do anything right? Will you help me?* (Tip: Each time a sentence is used, emphasize a different word in it. Example: I *am* so mad. I am *so* mad. I am so *mad.* I am so mad. Discuss the differences with the children. Now the students should be ready to work on the script, keeping the above expressive activities in mind.

Get Set (Practice! Practice! Practice!)

1. Script Familiarity—Give each child a script, and allow time for the children to read the script silently. You may want to read the script aloud, playing all the roles and using different voices for each part, to demonstrate what could be done. You may also want to paraphrase the story and talk about it. Think of how the characters would look, act, and sound as they say certain lines. Discuss the emotions (if any) behind some of the lines. Discuss the important role of the narrator, who introduces the play, provides narrative detail, and helps move the story along. The narrator should be a strong reader.

2. Group Read-through—Read the script round-robin style, beginning with the person on the teacher's left. This gives each child a chance to use different voices and gain confidence in their reading/speaking ability, and it gives the teacher a chance to discover individual capabilities. After the read-through, discuss the presentation, what was good, and what could be changed or added. Re-read the script, allowing the students to assume different parts. Follow this up with another discussion. This time, discuss vocal intonation, facial expressions, body gestures, and other features that could be incorporated.

3. Casting—Allow children to volunteer for the roles they're interested in. If students are hesitant to volunteer at first, assign the parts. Once cast, make sure each reader has a script that is highlighted for his/her part. Now read the script again, using the cast. After the reading, hold a discussion in which ideas on how a reader can improve intonation, pronunciation, or projection are suggested. When making suggestions, refer to the character's name rather than the name of the child playing the part. This makes it easier for a child to accept criticism. If enthusiasm is high and time permits, do another reading, using a new cast.

4. Staging—Go to the "performance" area (a separate room or portion of the classroom) and acquaint the cast with stage directions: *Upstage* (for minor parts) is away from the audience; *Downstage* (for main character) is toward the audience; *Stage Left* (narrator and/or lesser character) is the actor's left when facing the audience; *Stage Right* (narrator and/or lesser character) is the actor's right. Determine where the characters will stand or sit, and in what formation—line, semicircle, or staggered lines. Try to use varying levels to make it more interesting—some readers will stand, others may sit on the floor, pillows, short stools, chairs, or bar stools.

5. Rehearse—Once the characters are selected, they need to practice reading their parts several times. They also need to practice walking to their spot on stage, carrying their scripts. Because the narrators have the most lines to read, they could use a music stand for their scripts. Characters will hold their own scripts and remain on stage. As part of the reading, minor characters could step forward to read, then step back to position, and turn around when finished reading. There are some instances when a minor character could leave the stage area after reading his/her part. These actions should also be practiced. If props and costumes are being used, readers need to become comfortable with these, too.

6. Polish—Readers should practice in front of a small audience (the other members of the class). The audience has an important role and should react and applaud appropriately, giving the readers feedback. Later, the audience can be helpful in making suggestions regarding interpretation and projection. Readers should remain in character throughout the presentation, even when not reading lines. Readers need to focus on the audience, making sure their heads are up and their voices project. It isn't necessary to memorize the lines, but the reader should know them well enough to be able to read smoothly, pronouncing and interpreting effectively, and to glance up occasionally from the page. Here's where facial expressions are important. Characters may glance at each other while interacting, but the narrator should focus on the audience. Frequent practices will allow the readers to feel comfortable with their roles, bring the story to life, and

prepare to perform the story before others. Children not reading will follow along and become familiar with the story and possible interpretations.

7. What Else?—Although costumes, makeup, props, and sets aren't necessary, symbolic items can make the readers theatre presentation more interesting and fun. For example, a king could wear a crown; a stick could be a staff. A few props could be on stage to add atmosphere. Keep the extras simple; too much can be overwhelming to young readers. *At all times, remember that the emphasis of readers theatre is on the reading—nothing else really matters!*

Go! (Perform)

Once the story is secure, the children may enjoy presenting it to other classes, at an assembly program, for parents, or at local senior citizen residences and nursing homes. Performance space is any open area, with or without seating options. Be creative with the staging and meeting space availability and needs, as well as the needs of the readers. Although there is no specific staging, the narrator(s) is usually off to one side (or may be on opposite sides of the stage area), while the main character(s) may stand or sit front and center, and lesser characters are strategically placed on the stage area. If characters are not identified in the story, they may wear signs around their necks with the characters' names on them. Or, before beginning the story, you may want to consider having each reader step forward and tell his/her name and the role to be read. For example: **Narrator 1:** Hello, we would like to present (*name of story*). I am (*tell name*) and I am a narrator. **Narrator 2:** I am (*tell name*), also a narrator who will help tell the story. Characters would say, "I am (*name*) and I am (*the part*)."

The Finish (After the Presentation)

Now is the time for the entire class to discuss the story and the presentation. Talk about how the script enhanced the story, what could be added (or deleted), alternate dialogue suggestions, and different settings for the story. Consider the presentation, commenting on expressiveness, intonation, and projection, modifications or changes that could be made, and other suggestions that would enhance the presentation. File the script for future use, and begin the readers theatre process again with a new script. As more scripts are developed, students will know what to expect and do, and readers theatre will become easier. When several scripts have been developed, a full Readers Theatre Program or Festival would be fun to present to the PTA, organizations, and other classes in the school. Each script would have its own cast, and all students would be involved. The audience will enjoy seeing and hearing a variety of stories.

Create Your Own Readers Theatre Scripts

Once readers theatre has been introduced and used, students usually want more! There are several readers theatre books and scripts available (see Resources at the back of this book), but creating your own scripts is an adventure for the entire class. Besides reading new stories, children are free to use their imagination to create characters and dialogue. As students become familiar with the format of readers theatre, their writing skills are encouraged and enhanced. Original stories may also be used for readers theatre. There are no boundaries! The following are some suggestions for you and your students to think about. If students are going to write scripts, you may want to consider having them work with a partner, or in small groups.

What Will You Script?

Known stories from books are a good way to begin. How and why stories are plentiful, as are fairy tales, folk tales, legends, and myths, to name a few genres. Readers theatre scripts can impart information, moments in history, concepts, values, holiday material, biographical sketches, or anything else you or your class is interested in. Determine the reason for your script, find your material, review it, and make sure it's appropriate for your class. Students will find scripting after research to be a challenge, and the result will be rewarding.

Organize

After you have decided on what script to write and the information has been gathered, you need to put the material in a logical order. Envision the characters and the setting, and think about possible dialogue and action, as well as what the narrator(s) will say. Remember that the narrator secures the place of the story and the advancement of time, and helps identify the characters and what they are feeling and thinking.

Write

Use vocabulary and sentence structure that is appropriate for your grade level and class. Dialogue should be realistic, reflecting the way children talk. Keep the sentences short and simple. Write as many parts as you can, without going overboard and overcrowding the stage area. No more than ten characters is a good rule of thumb. That includes the narrator(s), one or two main characters, and several minor ones. Try to balance the roles—don't overload any one character with too many lines to read. Make the length of the script appropriate for your class. Shorter is good for young readers, while longer scripts are effective for more mature readers.

Try it Out

Run enough copies for the entire class, and begin reading it through. The techniques mentioned earlier should be applied, i.e., reading, analyzing, discussing, casting, practicing, and performing. If desired, rewrite the script, creating new characters, dialogue, situations, and so forth.

Keep Going

Use the same script to allow all students to participate. Then, start again with a new subject or story. Ask the students what they would like to work on next, then create a new one. Besides your classroom, let the students go on tour throughout the school and community. Videotaping readers theatre presentations is a good opportunity for the students to see and hear themselves in action!

Points to Remember

Readers theatre scripts can be short and sweet. They do *not* have to be perfectly structured (you're not writing for Broadway!) The simpler the script, the better it will be for you and your students. It is also not necessary to spend a lot of class time working on the script—several short sessions (ten to fifteen minutes each) is sufficient. Throughout the entire process of thinking, finding, creating, writing, and reading, have *fun!*

Final Thoughts on Readers Theatre

As introductory material to each script with this book, I've provided suggestions for presentation, props, and delivery. These are merely ideas for you to consider. Use your creativity, and that of your students, to develop your own staging, props, and delivery. Always remember that expressive reading is what is most important in readers theatre.

Readers theatre material is plentiful and without limits. Besides helping children enhance their reading skills, develop expressive oral skills, and increase their self-esteem and self-confidence, children have fun! Could a teacher ask for more?

How and Why Stories
for Readers Theatre

Why the Squirrel Lives in Trees

Summary

A wolf and a dog fight over who has the strongest teeth. When their friends join them, a cat does what the dog asks, and grabs the bear by the throat. Bear runs away in pain. Squirrel, fearing for his safety, runs up a tree and remains there. This is a Finnish tale. RL1

Presentation Suggestions

The narrators could stand on opposite sides of the stage area. The animals could be arranged across the stage, with the wolf and dog standing together. Cat should stand on the other side of the dog, and the bear should stand next to the cat. The other animals should stand in a small cluster in this order: squirrel, fox, rabbit.

Props

If desired, a cardboard tree could stand off to one side. The animals could wear ears and/or tails to represent them.

Delivery

Have the characters try to use different, contrasting voices for their parts. Bear's voice should be the deepest one.

Related Books

Bare, Colleen Stanley. *Busy, Busy Squirrels*. New York: Crown Publishing, 1989.
Jensen, Patricia. *Little Squirrel's Special Nest*. Pleasantville, NY: Reader's Digest, 1993.
Main, Margaret. *The Squirrel*. New York: Dial Books, 1981.
Mathews, Judith. *There's Nothing to D-o-o-o!* San Diego, CA: Harcourt, 1999.

Characters

Narrator 1
Narrator 2
Wolf

Dog
Cat
Bear
Fox
Rabbit
Squirrel

Why the Squirrel Lives in Trees

Narrator 1: Many years ago, the wolf and the dog were best friends. Wolf lived in the woods, and dog lived on a farm. Every day they would play together.

Narrator 2: One day, while they were playing, the wolf showed his teeth to the dog.

Wolf: Look, Dog. My teeth are better than yours. They're longer.

Dog: Your teeth may be longer, but *my* teeth are stronger. I think my teeth are better than yours.

Narrator 1: They argued about which had the best teeth.

Narrator 2: After a long time, Dog had an idea.

Dog: Wolf, go get your friends from the woods, and I'll get my friends from the farm. Come back with your friends when the sun is over the treetops.

Wolf: And then what will we do?

Dog: We'll fight to see who has the strongest teeth.

Narrator 1: Wolf went to the woods and got his friends Bear, Fox, Rabbit, and Squirrel.

Narrator 2: Dog went to the farm and got his friends Cow, Pig, Sheep, and Cat. Before they left the farm, Dog told Cat what he wanted her to do.

Dog: I need your help, Cat. Bear will be there. He's the biggest and strongest animal, so I want you to jump at him and catch his throat. Then he won't be able to hurt anyone.

Cat: Don't worry, friend. You can count on me!

Narrator 1: When the sun was over the treetops, all of the animals met. Cat did what Dog asked and caught Bear's throat.

Bear: *Owwww.* That hurts! Help! Help!

Narrator 2: Bear was in pain. He wanted to fight but couldn't because Cat wouldn't let go.

Bear: Help! Help! Someone help me!

Narrator 1: But no one came to help Bear. Bear jumped around, waving his big paws in the air. Finally, he broke loose and ran away into the woods.

Fox: Look! Bear is running away!

Rabbit: Bear is afraid!

Wolf: Don't run away, Bear! I need you.

Squirrel: If Bear is afraid and running away, I'll run, too!

Narrator 2: Squirrel quickly ran to a tree. He ran up the trunk, all the way to the top.

Narrator 1: Squirrel thought that if the smallest animal on the farm could fight the biggest animal in the woods, he had better get into the tree.

Squirrel: I'm not safe on the ground, but I am safe in this tree. I think I'll stay here for a while.

Narrator 2: Squirrel stayed in the tree for a long time. He was afraid to come down. In fact, to this day, squirrel still lives in a tree.

Why the Mouse Has a Seam in Its Face

Summary

Noah arranges two of every animal on his ark, and puts the mice next to the cats. When Cat sees the mice, he chases one into a hole. Cat tries to reach it with his paw. Mouse bites the paw, and Cat scratches the mouse's face. Noah repairs the scratch, and a thin seam remains. This is a Jewish folktale. RL1

Presentation Suggestions

The narrators could be split, with one on each side of the stage. Noah should be in the center, with Cat and Mouse near by.

Props

Noah could wear a robe with a rope around the waist. The cat could have a tail pinned to his backside, and the mouse could have short, gray ears on a headband. Both the mouse and cat could have whisker lines painted on their faces.

Delivery

Mouse should have a high, squeaky voice, while cat's voice should be in a lower range.

Related Books

Bogacki, Tomasz. *Cat and Mouse in the Night.* New York: Scholastic, 1990.
Chottin, Ariane. *Little Mouse's Rescue.* Pleasantville, NY: Reader's Digest, 1993.
Lobel, Arnold. *Mouse Tales.* New York: HarperCollins, 1972.

Characters

Narrator 1
Narrator 2
Noah
Cat
Mouse

Why the Mouse Has a Seam in Its Face

Narrator 1: Noah gathered together two of every animal and loaded them onto his ark. He found a place for each one.

Noah: Elephants, I want you in the back. Monkeys, you can hang from the beams. Mice, you can sit next to the Cats. But be quiet—the cats are tired and now they're sleeping.

Narrator 2: The mice quietly crept beside one of the cats, and settled down to take a nap. Just as they closed their eyes, Cat woke up. He opened one eye and saw the mice.

Cat: Am I dreaming, or do I really see mice?

Narrator 1: Cat remembered when his father had chased mice. And when his father caught them, he ate them.

Cat: Dad said mice taste *very* good! Well, if they were good enough for Dad, they should be good for me, too.

Narrator 2: Cat jumped at one of the mice, and his paw landed on her.

Mouse: *Eeek!* A cat! I must run! I must hide! I can't let him catch me!

Narrator 1: Mouse ran as fast as her short little legs could go. Cat chased the mouse, running quickly and with long strides.

Cat: Come back here! Quit zigging and zagging all over the place.

Mouse: No way! I don't want to be your supper!

Narrator 2: Mouse found a small hole and rushed inside. Her heart raced, and she panted. Finally, she was able to relax a little bit.

Mouse: Whew! That was close! Too close for comfort.

Narrator 1: Cat reached the hole and tried to get into it. First he poked his nose in. Then he tried to stick in his paws, one by one. But it was no use—he was too big.

Cat: Come on out, Mouse. I won't hurt you. I only want to play with you. We could be great friends.

Mouse: Hah! I don't believe you, Cat. You don't want to play with me. You want to eat me!

Narrator 2: Of course, Mouse was right. Cat *did* want to eat her.

Narrator 1: Cat put a paw into the hole again, hoping that this time he would be able to reach the mouse.

Narrator 2: But when Mouse saw Cat's paw, she opened her mouth *very* wide. Unable to see where his paw was going, Cat put it into the mouth of the mouse.

Narrator 1: Mouse bit down as hard as she could on Cat's paw. That hurt Cat very much, and Cat yelled loudly.

Cat: *YEEOOWWW!*

Narrator 2: Cat swiped at Mouse's cheek with his sharp claws, and Mouse let go of Cat right away.

Narrator 1: Cat pulled his paw out and slinked away so he could care for his hurt paw.

Narrator 2: When Mouse thought it was safe, she came out and scurried to Noah. Mouse showed Noah the long scratch on her cheek.

Mouse: Look what Cat did to me, Noah! Cat scratched me on my face, and it hurts. Can you fix it for me?

Narrator 1: Noah took a hair from the tail of one of the pigs and sewed up the tear in the mouse's cheek.

Noah: There, that should take care of you. Now you'll be as good as new.

Narrator 2: The tear was fixed and Mouse was happy.

Narrator 1: But if you look closely at the face of a mouse, you will see a thin line in the cheek next to its mouth. And now you know why.

How the Dog Got His Wet, Cold Nose

Summary

Because Dog is the last to enter Noah's ark, there is little space for him and his nose remains outside in the rain and cold. This is a Jewish folktale. RL1

Presentation Suggestions

The narrators could stand beside each other in the front off to one side. Noah should stand in the center, while the other animals should be on the opposite side from the narrators. Dog should walk toward Noah and read his part from center stage.

Props

To help identify the various animals when they speak, each character could wear a sign around his/her neck with the name of the animal on it.

Delivery

Think in terms of different animal voices for variation. Giraffe could speak in a loud stage whisper, Horse's voice could have a neighing quality, while Dog's voice could have a barking quality.

Related Books

Baynes, Pauline. *How Dog Began*. New York: Henry Holt & Co., 1987.
Cole, William. *Have I Got Dogs!* New York: Viking Press, 1993.
Hansard, Peter. *Wag, Wag, Wag*. Cambridge, MA: Candlewick Press, 1994.

Characters

Narrator 1
Narrator 2
Noah
Goat 1
Goat 2
Horse 1

Horse 2
Giraffe 1
Giraffe 2
Dog 1
Dog 2

How the Dog Got His Wet, Cold Nose

Narrator 1: Have you ever noticed how a dog's nose is cold and wet? Well, it wasn't always that way. A long, long time ago, a dog's nose was warm and dry.

Narrator 2: But then, when Noah built his ark, things changed.

Noah: Finally! After all these years, my ark is finished. Now I must get two of every animal and put them on the ark.

Narrator 1: It took a long time, but at last, Noah had the animals on board.

Noah: Before I close the doors, I'll make sure I have two of everything. When you hear me call you, please answer. Goats.

Goat 1: We're here, Noah.

Noah: Horses.

Horse 1: Over here.

Noah: Giraffes.

Giraffe 1: Here.

Giraffe 2: Me, too.

Noah: Yes, I see you standing at the back.

Narrator 2: As Noah called the roll, each animal answered.

Narrator 1: Then he called for the dogs.

Noah: Dogs. *Dogs.* DOGS! Where are the dogs?

Dog 1: I'm here, Noah, but I don't know where my mate is.

Narrator 2: Noah asked if any of the animals had seen the other dog.

Noah: Goat, have you seen the dog?

Goat 2: No I haven't, Noah. And I'm packed in so tightly, I can't even look around for him.

Noah: Giraffe, you're tall. Do you see the dog?

Giraffe 1: No, Noah, I don't see him anywhere.

Noah: Maybe the dog didn't get on the ark. Horse, run out and see if you can find the dog. Be quick. The sky is getting dark and soon it will rain. Bring him back before it does.

Horse 2: I'll go right away, Noah.

Narrator 2: Horse ran out the door of the ark and galloped off. Soon, he returned with the dog on his back.

Noah: Good job, Horse. You beat the rain. Dog, get onto the ark—now!

Dog 2: Where do you want me to stand? All the animals are shoulder to shoulder. There isn't any room for me.

Narrator 1: Noah looked at the animals. They stood close together. Then he had an idea.

Noah: When I count to three, I want all of you to take a deep breath. Ready? One. Two. Three.

Narrator 2: All of the animals took a deep breath . . .

All Animals: (*suck in breath and hold it*)

Narrator 1: . . . and the dog backed up into a space near the door.

Noah: Now we're ready to go. Stand back while I close the door.

Narrator 2: But just as Noah was ready to close the door, the animals could no longer hold their breath, and they all let it out.

All Animals: (*blow breath out*)

Narrator 1: Dog was pushed forward so part of him was outside the ark.

Narrator 2: By now it was raining hard, and the ark began to move. Noah closed the door.

Narrator 1: But Dog's nose was still outside!

Dog 2: Hey! What about me?

Noah: Sorry, Dog, we have to go. Make the best of it. A little rain won't hurt you.

Narrator 2: It rained for forty days and forty nights.

Dog 2: My nose is getting wet. And it is sooo cold!

Narrator 1: And that's why, to this day, dogs have a wet, cold nose.

Narrator 2: And that is also why dogs like to put their head out the window of a moving car.

Why the Fox Has White on the Tip of His Tail

Summary

An old woman seeks help caring for her sheep and cows. She rejects the offers of a bear and wolf but is impressed with the fox and his smooth ways. Later, the old woman discovers that some of her animals are missing, and learns that the fox has tricked her. She chases him and throws a pail of milk at him, which lands on the end of his tail. This is a European tale. RL1

Presentation Suggestions

The narrators could be split, with one on each side of the staging area. The old woman should stand in the center, with the animals close to her. The fox should stand nearest to the old woman and slightly behind her. When the fox reads, he could step forward, then step back into place when finished. The other animals should stand slightly apart from the old woman.

Props

The old woman could wear a bandana on her head. The fox could have a bushy tail pinned to his back. If desired, a pail with torn-up paper inside could be placed next to the old woman. When the narrator reads that the old woman throws the milk, she could pick up the pail and toss the paper at the fox.

Delivery

Think of vocal qualities for the characters. The old woman could have a shaky, gravely voice. The bear's voice could be deep and growly. The fox should sound smooth, sly, and cunning.

Related Books

Aylesworth, Jim. *The Tale of Tricky Fox.* New York: Scholastic, 2001.
Bodnar, Judit Z. *Tale of a Tail.* New York: Lothrop Publishing, 1998.
Havard, Christian. *The Fox, Playful Prowler.* Watertown, MA: Charlesbridge Publishing, 1995.
Koralek, Jenny. *The Friendly Fox.* Boston, MA: Little, Brown & Co., 1998.

Characters

Narrator 1
Narrator 2
Old Woman
Bear
Wolf
Fox

Why the Fox Has White on the Tip of His Tail

Narrator 1: There was once an old woman who lived on a farm with her cows and sheep.

Narrator 2: Because she was old, she tired easily and could not do all of her work.

Old Woman: I need help. Perhaps I can find a boy who would help me.

Narrator 1: She walked down the road and soon met Bear.

Bear: Where are you going, Old Woman?

Old Woman: I'm looking for a boy to help me take care of my cows and sheep.

Bear: You don't have to look any further. I could help you.

Old Woman: Maybe you could. But first you must show me how you would call them.

Narrator 2: Bear opened his mouth and growled a long, deep growl.

Bear: *GRRROOOWWWLLL!*

Old Woman: Oh, my! That will never do. It would only scare them and they would be sure to run away.

Narrator 1: The Old Woman turned and walked away from Bear. Soon she met Wolf.

Wolf: Good day, Old Woman. Where are you going?

Old Woman: I'm looking for a boy to help me take care of my cows and sheep.

Wolf: I could help you.

Old Woman: Maybe you could. Show me how you would call them.

Narrator 2: Wolf threw back his head with his nose high in the air and began to howl.

Wolf: *AAHHOOOO!*

Old Woman: No, No! That will never do. It would only scare them and they would surely run away.

Narrator 1: Again, the Old Woman went down the road until she met Fox.

Fox: Hello, Old Woman. Where are you going?

Old Woman: I'm looking for a boy to help me take care of my cows and sheep.

Fox: Why not let me help you?

Old Woman: First, show me how you would call them.

Narrator 2: Fox used his nicest voice to show her how he would sweetly call the cows and sheep.

Fox: Come to me, cows. Come to me, sheep.

Old Woman: That's very good. Come home with me. I think my cows and sheep will like you.

Fox: And I *know* I will like them!

Narrator 1: The Old Woman showed Fox what to do, and Fox did his job.

Narrator 2: But each day either a sheep or cow was missing.

Narrator 1: The Old Woman went to Fox.

Old Woman: For the past two nights, one of my animals has been missing. I want to know why.

Fox: The first night a bear came and ate one of your cows. The second night a wolf came from the woods and ate a sheep.

Old Woman: That's terrible! Please look after my animals better so this will not happen again.

Fox: I do the best I can. I run up and down watching them all day. I guess I got tired and fell asleep.

Old Woman: Well, don't go to sleep again!

Narrator 2: The next day, the Old Woman thought about what Fox had said.

Old Woman: I may have been too hard on Fox. I guess all of his running must make him thirsty. I'll put some milk into a pail and bring it to him.

Narrator 1: But when she got to Fox, she saw that he was eating one of her sheep.

Old Woman: So, it was you who killed my cow and sheep!

Narrator 2: When Fox heard the Old Woman, he started to run away.

Narrator 1: The Old Woman ran after him, still carrying her pail of milk. When she got close to Fox, she threw the milk at him.

Narrator 2: Some of the milk landed on the end of his tail. And ever since then, the tip of Fox's tail has been white.

Why Bears Have Short Tails

Summary

This tale, which has two origin credits (Iroquois and Norway), tells how Bear, following Fox's advice, uses his long, bushy tail to go ice fishing. But when he tries to pull up the fish he thinks he caught, his tail is frozen in the ice. Bear pulls very hard, and his beautiful tail snaps off, resulting in a short, stubby tail. RL1

Presentation Suggestions

The two narrators could be split, with one on each side of the staging area. The bear and fox should be centrally located. All characters should stand.

Props

A string with paper fish clipped to it could be placed on the floor; the fox could pick it up and sling it around his neck when the narrator says that the fox grabbed the string of fish.

Delivery

Bear should have a deep voice. Fox's voice should sound smooth and cunning.

Related Books

Bruchac, Joseph. *Iroquois Stories—Heroes and Heroines, Monsters and Magic*. Freedom, CA: Crossing Press, 1985.

Hamilton, Martha, and Mitch Weiss. *How & Why Stories*. Little Rock, AR: August House, 1999.

Wildsmith, Brian. *Bear's Adventure*. New York: Pantheon, 1982.

Characters

Narrator 1

Narrator 2

Fox

Bear

Why Bears Have Short Tails

Narrator 1: Long ago, Bear had a beautiful, long bushy tail. But, if you look at Bear now, you'll see that he has a short, stubby tail.

Narrator 2: Let us tell you how that happened.

Narrator 1: One day, Fox was walking through the woods looking for food.

Fox: I'm so hungry, my stomach is growling. I feel weak!

Narrator 2: Fox headed for the river.

Fox: Maybe I'll find some fish to eat.

Narrator 1: But when he reached the river, it was covered with ice.

Fox: Oh, no! Now I won't find any fish.

Narrator 2: As he looked across the river, Fox saw a man sitting on the ice.

Narrator 1: The man was fishing. Lying on the ice next to him was a long string of fish.

Fox: I wish I could take that string of fish. Then I would have plenty to eat. But how can I get it?

Narrator 2: Just then, the man got up and walked away, leaving the string of fish on the ice.

Narrator 1: When Fox could no longer see the man, he ran across the ice, grabbed the string of fish, and ran back to the woods.

Narrator 2: Along the way, Fox met Bear. Bear saw the string of fish on Fox's back.

Bear: Hey, Fox, where did you get all those fish?

Fox: I caught them in the river.

Bear: You can't fool me, Fox. The river is covered with ice.

Fox: I know, but I cut a hole in the ice. Then I dropped my long, bushy tail into the water. The fish nibbled a bit, then hung on to my tail. When I had enough fish, I yanked my tail from the water. And there they were!

Narrator 1: Bear was amazed.

Bear: I love fish! Do you think I could catch some with my tail?

Narrator 2: Fox looked at Bear's long, bushy tail.

Fox: I don't see why not. I must warn you, Bear. The water will be very cold, but you'll get used to it. Then you will feel some stings. Don't mind that. It's just the fish biting. The longer you hold your tail in the water, the more fish you'll get. Then, when you think you have enough, pull your tail from the water.

Narrator 1: Fox told Bear where to find the hole in the ice and warned him to be careful when he walked across the river.

Narrator 2: Bear thanked Fox and ran to the river and saw the hole.

Narrator 1: Bear carefully walked to the hole and dropped his tail into it.

Bear: *Brrr. Brrr.* Fox was right. This water is *very* cold!

Narrator 2: But soon the cold didn't bother Bear any more. Then he felt a sting.

Bear: Oh! A fish just bit my tail! There's another one! I think Fox was smart. This is a good way to catch fish.

Narrator 1: Bear sat over the hole for a long time. Every now and then, he felt a sting. He was sure he was catching many fish. His tail was freezing. Soon he felt nothing. He was numb.

Bear: I think I have enough fish now.

Narrator 2: Bear tried to stand, but his tail didn't come out of the water.

Narrator 1: Bear pulled again, this time harder. His tail still didn't come up.

Narrator 2: Bear pulled *very* hard. He heard a crack. Bear looked behind him. His tail had snapped off. His beautiful, long, bushy tail was now short. And that's why bears have short, stubby tails to this day.

Why Cats Always Wash Themselves after Eating

Summary

This European tale tells how a clever bird, who was about to be eaten by a cat, was able to escape. RL1

Presentation Suggestions

The narrators should stand to the front on opposite sides of the stage area. Cat should be in the center. Bird should stand near the cat, but with his back to him. Bird should turn to the audience when he reads his part. Bird can move to the tree when the narrator reads ". . . the bird quickly flew to the tops of a tree."

Props

A cardboard tree could be placed at one side of the stage. The cat could wear symbolic features (ears and/or tail) and the bird could wear a band of feathers.

Delivery

Cat should read with a slow, smooth, soft voice. Bird's voice should be high pitched. Be aware of what is being said, and use appropriate inflections to show the emotions expressed.

Related Books

Bonners, Susan. *Why Does the Cat Do That?* New York: Henry Holt & Co., 1998.
DeSpain, Pleasant. *Tales of Cats*. Little Rock, AR: August House, 2003.
Hamilton, Martha, and Mitch Weiss. *How & Why Stories*. Little Rock, AR: August House, 1999.

Characters

Narrator 1
Narrator 2
Cat
Bird

Why Cats Always Wash Themselves after Eating

Narrator 1: A hungry cat was looking for something to eat.

Cat: I am *so* hungry. But today I don't feel like eating a mouse. And I don't feel like eating fish. And I don't feel like drinking milk. Today, I want something special.

Narrator 2: As the cat walked, he looked around. Then he saw a little bird.

Cat: Ah! That little bird would be delicious! He's plump and probably would be quite juicy! That's exactly what I want.

Narrator 1: The bird was busy digging for worms for his own dinner. He didn't see or hear the cat sneak up on him. Then suddenly . . .

Cat: Gotcha!

Narrator 2: The cat held the bird tightly in its paws. The poor little bird was so scared, he couldn't move or think.

Cat: Hello, little bird. You are very cute. And it looks like you've been eating a lot of fat, juicy worms.

Narrator 1: The cat teased the bird.

Bird: Why did you catch me, Mr. Cat? What do you want with me?

Cat: Want with you? Why, I want to be your friend. We can play together.

Narrator 2: The cat tossed the bird back and forth between his paws.

Bird: Oh, please, Mr. Cat. Let me go.

Cat: Let you go? Well . . . all right. I'll let you go.

Narrator 1: The cat pushed the bird into one paw.

Cat: Nope. I changed my mind. I think we should have dinner together. You eat your worm, then I'll eat you!

Narrator 2: Then the cat pushed the bird into the other paw. By now the little bird once again had his breath and wits.

Bird: I see. Are you going to eat me now?

Cat: Yes, that is what I plan to do. And it will do you no good to argue with me.

Bird: I'm not arguing. But I must admit, I am a bit disappointed.

Cat: Disappointed? What do you mean, you're disappointed?

Bird: Well, it's bad enough to be eaten by a cat. But it's even worse to be eaten by a cat that has no manners.

Narrator 1: Now it was the cat's turn to get upset.

Cat: What do you mean I have no manners?

Bird: I've been in many places and have seen lots and lots of cats. And everywhere, cats *always* wash before eating. It's the only polite thing to do. Besides, you don't want to eat all the dirt that's on your paws, do you?

Narrator 2: The cat was insulted.

Cat: Of course not! And I know you're supposed to wash before eating. I *always* wash first. I just forgot!

Narrator 1: To prove his point, the cat let go of the bird and began to wash himself. He carefully licked each paw.

Cat: There, you see. I know how to do it properly. You can't tell me I have no manners.

Narrator 2: But while the cat was busy washing himself, the bird quickly flew to the top of a tree. Now he was safe from the cat.

Cat: Hey! Where are you going? Oh, no! You tricked me.

Narrator 1: And since then, cats always eat first and wash afterwards.

Why Bear Sleeps All Winter Long

Summary

Bear always plays tricks on Rabbit, but with the help of Fox and other friends, Rabbit plays a trick on Bear. This is based on a Native American story. RL1

Presentation Suggestions

Narrators could be together off to one side. The rabbit should be centrally located, with the other animals slightly behind. Consider having each animal step forward toward the rabbit as they are introduced and remain there until the end. Initially, the bear would be in the center with the rabbit but then go to one side after the narrators tell about the tricks he plays on the rabbit. Bear would remain at the side for the duration of the reading.

Props

If possible, use symbolic costumes for the animals: long ears for rabbit; long, bushy tail for fox; bushy tail for squirrel; long, thin tail for mole. Bear could wear a fur coat. A small, hollow log (real or rolled-up oak-tag or construction paper) could be placed on the side where Bear stands. One or two cardboard trees on the stage could help with the setting.

Delivery

Consider how each animal looks and might sound. Bear should have the deepest voice. The other animal voices should vary in pitch and volume. Squirrel and rabbit may want to speak a little faster than mole and frog. Frog's voice could have a croaking quality, and fox's voice could have a smooth, deliberate sound.

Related Books

Berger, Melvin. *Growl! A Book About Bears.* New York: Cartwheel Books, 1999.
Bittner, Wolfgang. *Wake Up, Grizzly!* New York: North-South Books, 1996.
Harrison, Annette. *Easy-to-Tell Stories for Young Children.* Jonesborough, TN: National Storytelling Press, 1992.
Wildsmith, Brian. *The Lazy Bear.* Danbury, CT: Franklin Watts, Inc., 1974.
Wilson, Karma. *Bear Snores On.* New York: Dial Books for Young Readers, 1984.

Characters

Narrator 1

Narrator 2

Squirrel

Rabbit

Bear

Frog

Mole

Fox

Why Bear Sleeps All Winter Long

Narrator 1: Squirrel worked hard and was always busy. She was *really* busy in the fall.

Squirrel: Soon it will be winter. Now I must find lots of nuts and bury them. Then, I'll have food when it snows and is cold.

Narrator 2: Fox was busy too. He looked after the chickens on a farm.

Narrator 1: Rabbit was also busy. She found food to store.

Rabbit: I'll pick cabbages and lettuce. I'll pull some turnips and carrots. Then, when winter comes, I'll have food to eat.

Narrator 2: Then there was Bear. In daytime, he found honey and went fishing. After that, he went to sleep in the warm sun. He didn't do much work.

Bear: This was a good day. I found honey and caught two fish. Now it's time to take my nap.

Narrator 1: When Bear was not napping, he liked to play tricks on the other animals. Mostly, he played tricks on Rabbit. Like this one—

Bear: I see that Rabbit has filled her tree stump with food! But Rabbit isn't here, so I'll hide her food.

Narrator 2: Bear took the food from Rabbit's stump and hid all of it.

Narrator 1: Another time, Bear messed up her stump.

Bear: Rabbit has nice, warm, dry leaves in her stump. She did a good job laying them around. I'll just stomp on them and kick them. When Rabbit comes home, she won't know what happened! This will be a good trick.

Narrator 2: Each time Bear played a trick on Rabbit, Rabbit got madder and madder.

Rabbit: I can't take it any more! Bear plays too many mean tricks on me. I don't know what to do! I can't keep Bear away by myself. I'll go ask my friends to help me.

Narrator 1: Rabbit hopped over to the pond to find Frog. Frog was sitting on a lily pad, soaking up the sun.

Rabbit: Frog, please help me. Bear is always tricking me, and it's not fair. Will you help me make him stop?

Frog: I don't know what I could do, but let's go see Squirrel. Maybe she can help.

Narrator 2: Frog and Rabbit went to see Squirrel. Squirrel was sitting in a tree, eating nuts.

Frog: Squirrel, Rabbit needs your help.

Rabbit: Yes, I do. Bear is always tricking me, and I want him to stop. Can you help me?

Squirrel: I don't think so, but I bet Mole could think of a way to help you. Let's go see him.

Narrator 1: So, Squirrel, Frog, and Rabbit went to see Mole. Mole was digging a new home for himself. The dirt was flying all over the place.

Squirrel: Mole, Rabbit needs your help.

Rabbit: Yes, I do. Bear is always tricking me and I don't like it. Can you make him stop?

Mole: Hmmm, I don't know what I could do. Let's go find Fox. He's the smart one—he'll think of some way to stop Bear.

Narrator 2: Now, Mole, Squirrel, Frog, and Rabbit went to find Fox. They found him behind a tree, brushing his bushy tail.

Mole: Fox, Rabbit needs your help.

Rabbit: I hope you can help me, Fox. Bear plays lots of tricks on me and I want him to stop. Do you think you can help me?

Fox: Hmmm. Maybe I can. Has anyone seen Bear today?

Rabbit: I haven't.

Frog: Not me.

Squirrel: Nope.

Mole: Not me.

Fox: Let's go find him.

Narrator 1: The animals followed Fox. They looked here. They looked there. They looked everywhere!

Fox: Here he is!

Narrator 2: Fox found Bear sleeping in a hollow log.

Fox: Shhh. Don't wake him up. Now, I know what to do. Frog, bring me some mud from your pond.

Frog: I'll hop to it right away!

Fox: Squirrel, bring me some leaves from your tree.

Squirrel: You got it! I'll be right back.

Fox: Mole, bring me some of your digging dirt.

Mole: I'll go as fast as I can.

Narrator 1: Soon the animals came back. Bear was still sleeping. Fox told the animals what to do.

Fox: Rabbit, fill Bear's log with mud from Frog's pond. Next, put in the leaves from Squirrel's tree. Then, put in the dirt from Mole's new hole.

Narrator 2: Rabbit did what Fox told her to. When the log was full, she used her hind legs to pack the mud, leaves, and dirt in tightly.

Narrator 1: The animals left and Bear was still sleeping. Each time he woke up, he saw that it was still dark.

Bear: What a long night this is. I'll go back to sleep until I see the sun.

Narrator 2: Bear slept all winter long. When he finally woke up, he felt great.

Bear: That was a good sleep! I feel *very* rested.

Narrator 1: He pushed the mud, leaves, and dirt out of the log. Then he walked out.

Bear: Birds are singing! Wildflowers are blooming! The sun is shining! My goodness, I slept all winter and now it's spring! I feel so great that I'm going to do this every year!

Narrator 2: Bear did what he said he would—every winter he slept until spring.

Narrator 1: Rabbit was happy, too. Bear never tricked her again, and she had time to play in the snow.

Narrator 2: And now you know why bears sleep all winter long.

How the Goat Lost His Tail

Summary

In spite of Noah's repeated warnings, Goat fails to get on the ark. When the rain pours, goat jumps on the ark just as Noah closes the door. This is a Jewish folktale. RL2

Presentation Suggestions

Consider having the narrators together off to one side. Noah should be in the center. The first goat should be near Noah, then step back or leave the area after reading. The second goat could be off to one side of the stage until he gets on the ark, at which time he would walk to the center near Noah.

Props

If possible, sound effects for the rain could be made by crunching cellophane or crisp paper.

Delivery

As Noah gets annoyed, this should be reflected in his voice. The second goat should read his "I know it" lines in a matter-of-fact way. The voices of the two goats should contrast, perhaps in pitch or volume.

Related Books

Bornstein, Ruth Lercher. *Of Course a Goat.* New York: HarperCollins, 1980.
Dunn, Judy. *The Little Goat.* New York: Random House, 1978.
Miller, Sara Swan. *Goats.* New York: Children's Press, 2000.

Characters

Narrator 1
Narrator 2
Noah
Goat 1
Goat 2

How the Goat Lost His Tail

Narrator 1: Noah collected two of every animal and was now loading them onto his ark. As they walked up the ramp, he checked them off of his list.

Narrator 2: At long last, all of the animals were settled on the ark. Goat was now ready to enter the ark, and Noah noticed that there was only one goat.

Noah: Where is the other goat?

Goat 1: He's still in the meadow nibbling on the grass.

Noah: What's he doing out there? Doesn't he know he should be getting on the ark?

Goat 1: I tried to tell him, Noah, but he wouldn't listen to me. Maybe he'll listen to you.

Narrator 1: Noah cupped both hands around his mouth and yelled.

Noah: Goat! Come here! All of the animals have obeyed except you.

Narrator 2: The stubborn goat heard Noah, but he didn't move. He continued to nibble the grass, while swishing his long tail back and forth.

Noah: Goat, did you hear me? I said all of the other animals are on the ark except you.

Narrator 1: Goat looked up from his nibbling and answered between chews.

Goat 2: I know it.

Narrator 2: Then Goat returned to eating the grass. This made Noah extremely angry.

Noah: Goat, I mean it! You need to get on the ark—*now.* Don't you see that big black cloud forming in the distance? Soon we'll have rain.

Goat: I know it.

Narrator 1: But Goat still didn't move. The big, black cloud covered the sky, which slowly became darker and darker. Noah tried calling to Goat again.

Noah: Look, Goat, you *must* get on the ark. We're running out of time. Now it's beginning to sprinkle.

Goat 2: I know it.

Narrator 2: Goat continued chewing the grass and the black cloud split open. A hard, driving rain fell.

Noah: Goat, it's pouring! I'm going to shut the door to the ark, and if you're not here when the door is closed, we'll have to leave without you.

Narrator 2: Noah couldn't wait for the goat and began to shut the door.

Narrator 1: Just as the door was about to be secured, Goat ran and jumped in.

Narrator 2: But he wasn't fast enough and the door cut off his tail.

Noah: Now, see what has happened to you? You don't have your beautiful tail anymore! In fact, you don't even have a tail!

Narrator 1: Goat looked behind him. When he saw what had happened to his tail, he was very sad, and all he could say was . . .

Goat 2: I know it.

Narrator 2: And ever since that day, all goats have hardly any tail at all.

Why Dogs Sniff

Summary

Dogs gather for a celebration, remove their tails, and hang them on the leaves of corn plants. A strange noise frightens them, and in their haste to get away, they grab any old tail. Later, they try to find the one that belongs to them. This is a Native American (Pima) tale. RL2

Presentation Suggestions

The two narrators could stand together off to one side, while the dogs could stand slightly off center, in a well-spaced group.

Props

A rope tail could be attached to each dog character.

Delivery

Because all of the characters are dogs, each should develop a different voice, varying pitch, volume, slight accent, and so forth.

Related Books

Baynes, Pauline. *How Dog Began.* New York: Henry Holt & Co., 1987.
Coffelt, Nancy. *The Dog Who Cried Woof.* San Diego, CA: Harcourt, 1995.
Winthrop, Elizabeth. *I'm the Boss!* New York: Holiday House, 1991.

Characters

Narrator 1
Narrator 2
Dog 1
Dog 2
Dog 3
Dog 4
Dog 5

Why Dogs Sniff

Narrator 1: There was once a time when dogs often gathered to celebrate events and to enjoy themselves.

Narrator 2: Their favorite place to meet was in the cornfield, where there was a lot of space.

Dog 1: Let's meet this afternoon and celebrate!

Dog 2: What are we celebrating?

Dog 1: Well, we've had a good year. The summer wasn't too hot, we had plenty of food, and now fall is here.

Dog 2: You're right. We have many reasons to celebrate.

Dog 1: So, spread the word—all dogs will meet in the cornfield when the sun is high in the sky.

Narrator 1: Word spread quickly, and by the time the sun was overhead, dogs from near and far had come to the cornfield.

Narrator 2: As the dogs arrived, they removed their tails and hung them up on the leaves of the corn plants. And the celebration began.

Dog 1: Let's dance!

Dog 2: Let's chase each other!

Dog 3: Let's sing!

Narrator 1: Of course the dogs couldn't sing, but they could howl and bark. And it became quite noisy!

Dogs: (*bark and howl*)

Narrator 2: The dogs had a wonderful time, when suddenly, one of them heard a noise and yelled to the others.

Dog 4: STOP! Did you hear that?

Dog 5: Hear what?

Dog 4: That noise. Listen.

Narrator 1: They all listened and heard a strange noise that came from the other side of the cornfield.

Dog 5: What is it?

Dog 4: I don't know, but I don't like the sound of it.

Dog 1: I'm scared!

Dog 2: Me too!

Dog 3: Let's get out of here—fast!

Narrator 2: The dogs ran over to the corn plants and grabbed any tail they could find.

Narrator 1: Then they hurried back to their village, where they made a terrible discovery.

Dog 1: Hey, this isn't my tail!

Dog 2: And this one isn't mine!

Narrator 2: One by one, all of the dogs realized that none of them had their own tail.

Narrator 1: They went to each other, sniffing the tails, trying to find the one that belonged to them.

Dog 3: (*sniffing*) Do you have my tail?

Dog 4: (*sniffing*) Is that *my* tail you have on?

Dog 5: (*sniffing*) I think I smell my tail, but where is it?

Narrator 2: And so to this day, many dogs still go around sniffing each other's tails because they want their own tail back.

Why Bat Flies Alone

Summary

When the animals and birds fight, the bat always goes with the winner, claiming to be one of them. Later, his deceptiveness is discovered, and neither the animals nor birds want to have anything to do with him. This is a tale from the Modoc Indians, but is also found in many European folktales, as well as Aesop's Fables. RL3

Presentation Suggestions

Narrators could be together off to one side. The animals should be grouped together, and the birds should be grouped together. Bat should stand between the two groups.

Props

The deer could have a headband with antlers. The animals and birds could be dressed in colors that represent them: black for the bat, red for the cardinal, blue for the blue jay, and brown for the bear.

Delivery

Bear should have a deep voice while the deer's voice could be in a more normal tone. The birds should have higher pitched voices.

Related Books

Cannon, Janell. *Stellaluna.* San Diego, CA: Harcourt, 1993.
Horowitz, Ruth. *Bat Time.* New York: Four Winds Press, 1991.
Markle, Sandra. *Outside and Inside Bats.* NY: Bradbury Press, 1991.

Characters

Narrator 1
Narrator 2
Bat
Deer

Bear
Cardinal
Blue Jay

Why Bat Flies Alone

Narrator 1: Once, long ago, the animals and birds had a *big* fight.

Narrator 2: No one knew what they were fighting about, but it must have been important because all of them were in the battle. Except for Bat. He wasn't on either side.

Bat: This fight is silly. They don't know why they're fighting. The birds are trying to beat the animals, but it looks like the animals are winning. I'll hide under this log and wait to see what happens.

Narrator 1: After a long time, the fighting was over, and the animals had won.

Bat: Good! Now I'll go with the animals.

Narrator 2: He left the log and joined the animals. But the animals didn't want Bat to go with them.

Deer: Where do you think you're going, Bat?

Bat: With you.

Bear: No you're not! You were fighting for the birds.

Bat: Indeed I was not! I'm not a bird. Look at me. I have teeth. Birds don't have teeth! Have you ever seen a bird with teeth?

Deer: No, come to think of it, I haven't. Very well, since you're not a bird, you can come with us.

Narrator 2: The other animals agreed to let Bat go with them. But later, the animals and birds had another battle.

Narrator 1: Bat fought on the side of the animals. The birds seemed to be winning, so Bat hid under a log and waited.

Narrator 2: After a long, hard battle, the birds won and headed home.

Bat: I'll go home with the birds. After all, they won the battle.

Narrator 1: But the birds didn't like it when Bat joined them.

Cardinal: What are you doing here?

Bat: Going home with you.

Blue Jay: No way! You were fighting against us.

Bat: Oh, but I'm not one of the animals. Look at me! I have wings. As I'm sure you know, animals don't have wings.

Cardinal: This is true. I guess you can come along with us.

Narrator 2: Later, when there was peace between the animals and birds, Deer and Cardinal were talking.

Deer: I need to ask you something about Bat. When the animals won the first battle, Bat went with the animals. He said he wasn't a bird because he has teeth.

Cardinal: Yet, when the birds won the next battle, Bat went with us. He said he wasn't an animal because he has wings.

Deer: You know, Cardinal, I think Bat was going from one side to the other so he could be with the winners.

Cardinal: How sneaky of him! I think we should let all the animals and birds know what Bat did.

Narrator 1: Cardinal told all the birds and Deer told all the animals how Bat had tricked them.

Narrator 2: They were all angry at Bat.

Deer: Bat, what you did was sneaky and unfair. The animals don't want you around them any more.

Cardinal: Neither do the birds. From now on, Bat, you will fly alone at night. Then no one has to see you and put up with you again.

Narrator 1: Bat was ashamed of himself, but there was nothing he could say or do to change their minds.

Narrator 2: Ever since then, Bat always flies alone at night.

Why Donkeys Have Long Ears

Summary

Based on an Italian folktale in which Adam names the animals in his garden, the donkey cannot remember his name. After many interruptions, Adam gets mad and pulls on the donkey's ears, while repeating his name. RL3

Presentation Suggestions

The two narrators could stand beside each other to one side, while the animals are grouped in staggered formation on the opposite side. Adam should stand in the center. The donkey could approach Adam each time he reads and return to the animal group when he's finished.

Props

Each reader could wear something to represent his/her animal: Donkey in gray, with a rope tail; Giraffe in light yellow or tan, with brown spots pinned on; Elephant in gray, with large floppy ears and/or a trunk secured with elastic; Kangaroo in tan, with a carpenter's apron tied around the waist.

Delivery

Think in terms of the size and characteristics of the animals for vocalizations. Donkey could read his lines in an unsure, confused manner. Giraffe, who has a long neck, should use a stage whisper. Elephant's voice should be deeper than the other animals, while Kangaroo's voice could be a little higher pitched and rather bouncy. Adam's annoyance should grow gradually, until, at the end, he is yelling his lines.

Related Books

Berger, Barbara Helen. *The Donkey's Dream*. New York: Philomel, 1986.
Cohen, Barbara. *The Donkey's Story*. New York: Lothrop Publishing, 1988.
Duvoism, Roger Antoine. *Donkey, Donkey*. Berkeley, CA: Parent's Press, 1968.

Characters

Narrator 1
Narrator 2
Adam
Donkey
Giraffe
Elephant
Kangaroo

Why Donkeys Have Long Ears

Narrator 1: In the beginning of time, there was a man named Adam. As he walked through his garden, he passed different animals.

Narrator 2: He stopped, looked at them, and gave each one a name. He came to a gray animal with a long tail.

Adam: Now, what shall I call you? How about Donkey? Yes, I like that. Your name will be Donkey.

Donkey: That's a good name, Adam. I like it.

Narrator 1: Soon, Adam came to an animal with a long neck and skinny legs.

Adam: You are not like the other animals. I must give you a very special name. Let me see . . .

Narrator 2: Before Adam could think of a name, Donkey came to him.

Donkey: Excuse me, Adam. What did you say my name was?

Adam: Your name is Donkey.

Narrator 1: Adam turned back to the long-necked animal.

Adam: I know. I will call you Giraffe. That's a good name for an interesting animal.

Giraffe: Thank you, Adam. That's an unusual name.

Narrator 2: The next animal Adam came to was a very big one. It had a little tail behind and a big, long trunk in front.

Adam: You are indeed different, so I must think of a remarkable name for you. Hmmm . . .

Narrator 1: While Adam was thinking of a name for this big animal, Donkey came to him again.

Donkey: Sorry to bother you again, Adam, but I've forgotten the name you gave me.

Adam: Donkey. Your name is Donkey.

Donkey: Oh, yeah. Donkey. Donkey. Donkey. I'll try to remember that.

Narrator 2: Adam turned back to the big animal in front of him.

Adam: How do you like the name Elephant?

Elephant: I like it just fine, Adam. Thank you.

Narrator 1: Soon Adam saw an animal hopping around on its hind legs. It used its two short legs to help push itself off the ground. And it had a pocket on the front of its body.

Narrator 2: Adam decided to call him Kangaroo.

Kangaroo: Ooo, ooo, I like Kangaroo. And for this name, I thank you.

Adam: Not a bad poem, Kangaroo.

Narrator 1: As Kangaroo hopped away, Donkey came running up to Adam.

Donkey: I just can't seem to remember my name, Adam. What was it again?

Narrator 2: Adam got mad and was no longer calm. He put his hands on Donkey's ears and pulled as hard as he could. He yelled into Donkey's ears.

Adam: Donkey! *Donkey!* Your name is DONKEY!

Narrator 1: Donkey yelled with pain. Each time Adam said "Donkey," the ears grew longer, until they became as long as they are today.

Narrator 2: And that's why donkeys have long ears.

How Serval Got His Spots

Summary

Serval is unhappy with his drab looks, until Puff Adder rewards him with a handsome coat for nursing Puff Adder back to health. This is a Ndebele fable from Africa. RL3

Presentation Suggestions

Because there are so few characters, they could all be centrally located across the front. The narrators should be close together, off center. Leave a space so that Serval and Puff Adder can stand close together.

Props

Serval could be dressed in tan. When he gets his spots, a few black spots could be quickly placed on his clothing by Puff Adder, using double-faced tape or Velcro.

Delivery

To show contrast between the two characters, Serval could speak with a slightly growly voice, while Puff Adder could draw out his lines, especially those that have an "s".

Related Books

Arnosky, Jim. *Little Lion.* New York: Putnam, 1998.
Greaves, Nick. *When Lion Could Fly and Other Tales from Africa.* Hauppauge, NY: Barron's, 1993.
Presencer, Alain. *Roaring Lion Tales.* New York: HarperCollins, 1984.
Vogel, Elizabeth. *Big Cats—Lions.* New York: PowerKids Press, 2002.
Yoshida, Toshi. *Young Lions.* New York: Putnam, 1989.

Characters

Narrator 1
Narrator 2
Serval
Puff Adder

How Serval Got His Spots

Narrator 1: Serval, a large wildcat from Africa, was once a beautiful tawny color.

Narrator 2: You know, tannish yellow, like a lion.

Narrator 1: He *looked* like a lion, but he was much smaller and not as strong as a lion. The other animals often teased him and called him "Lion's Little Cousin."

Serval: I don't mind being Lion's cousin, but I don't like the way I look. Tan is such a drab color. I wish I had a grand coat with stripes like Zebra, or spots like Leopard. If I can't be big and strong, at least I could be handsome.

Narrator 2: One day, Serval was out hunting for food when he met Puff Adder, a deadly snake.

Narrator 1: Puff Adder was big, with a thick body and long fangs. But on this day, he looked small and weak.

Puff Adder: Oh, kind Serval, I'm glad to see you. I'm feeling very sick and don't know what to do. None of the other animals will help me.

Serval: No wonder! All of the animals know how nasty you are, and they're all afraid of you. They know that one bite from your long fangs will kill them.

Puff Adder: I admit that I haven't been very nice, but now I need help. Will you help me? Please?

Serval: I can see that you aren't well, so I will help you. But you must promise to keep your fangs to yourself. Don't even *try* to bite me.

Puff Adder: I promise—you won't even see my fangs.

Narrator 1: So, Serval took Puff Adder home and looked after him.

Narrator 2: It took a long time, but finally Puff Adder got better. Thanks to the care that Serval gave him, Puff Adder was well enough to leave Serval and go back to his own home.

Puff Adder: You've been very kind, Serval, and I'm grateful to you. Without your good care, I'm sure that I would have died.

Serval: I'm glad I was able to help you, Puff Adder. Now, go to your home. Maybe we'll meet each other again.

Puff Adder: And if we do, I promise I won't hurt you. To show you how grateful I am, I'll give you anything you want, as long as it's in my power to do so. What do you wish?

Serval: I've always wanted a beautiful coat. Do you think you can do that for me?

Puff Adder: Yes, I can do that. But I'll have to bite you first.

Serval: What? Bite me? Why? If you bite me, I will surely die.

Puff Adder: No, you won't die. I'll bite you gently and give you only a small amount of my poison. Trust me, it will not harm you.

Narrator 1: Puff Adder bit Serval carefully. It made Serval feel a little sick, but he quickly got better.

Narrator 2: Soon Serval's skin broke out in a rash. His tawny coat changed to a golden color with black spots all over it.

Serval: Look at me! My coat is beautiful! Now I am one of the most handsome creatures in the bush!

Narrator 1: Ever since then, Puff Adder and Serval live in the bush of Africa. They have respect for each other, and do not bother one another.

Narrator 2: And, Serval remembers that it was Puff Adder who gave him his beautiful spots.

How the Camel Got Its Proud Look

Summary

Upon request, the camel gets large, flat feet and humps on his back so that he can live in the desert. Because other animals tease him about his appearance, the camel asks for a superior look so that other animals will feel inferior and stop teasing him. This tale is thought to be from China. RL4

Presentation Suggestions

Both narrators should stand together off to one side. Camel should stand in the center, and Lord of Heaven should stand on the other side of the stage. When Camel speaks to the Lord of Heaven, they could move toward each other or each take a step forward. Consider having the three animals enter, read their lines, and then leave. Camel should look superior at the end.

Props

If possible, have the Lord of Heaven tie a pillow onto Camel's back when he gets his hump.

Delivery

Camel's voice should be soft. Lord of Heaven's voice should be strong. The three animals should have three distinct voices for variation.

Related Books

Arnold, Caroline. *Camel*. New York: Morrow Jr. Books, 1992.
Garcia, Eulalia. *Camels—Ships of the Desert*. Milwaukee, WI: Garrett Stevens, 1996.
Kipling, Rudyard. *How the Camel Got His Hump*. New York: HarperCollins, 1985.
Rubinetti, Donald. *Cappy the Lonely Camel*. New York: Silver Press, 1996.

Characters

Narrator 1
Narrator 2
Camel
Lord of Heaven (Lord)

Animal 1
Animal 2
Animal 3

How the Camel Got Its Proud Look

Narrator 1: In the beginning of time, the Lord of Heaven created all the animals, including the camel, which looked very much like other animals. There was nothing special or outstanding about him.

Narrator 2: One day, the camel started to walk out into the desert, which, of course, was all sand.

Camel: This is hard to walk in. My feet sink into the sand, and I don't get very far.

Narrator 1: So, the camel returned to the Lord of Heaven and complained.

Camel: The desert is so beautiful, and I really like it. In fact, I'd like to live in the desert. But when I try to walk in the sand, my four small feet sink into it and stick. Do you think you could make my feet so they'll carry me over the desert?

Lord: Of course I can. Just leave it to me. I'm delighted to know that you like my desert so much that you want to live there.

Narrator 2: Lord of Heaven reshaped the camel's feet and made them large and flat.

Lord: That should do it. See if you can walk in the sand better now.

Narrator 1: The camel went back into the desert and found that he could walk in the sand very easily.

Camel: This is great! Now my feet don't sink in the sand and get stuck. I can walk over the sand!

Narrator 2: Camel was very pleased with himself and walked proudly over the sand. But he had not gone far when he became very hungry and thirsty.

Camel: This is terrible! I need to see what Lord of Heaven can do about my hunger and thirst.

Narrator 1: So Camel returned to Lord of Heaven a second time.

Camel: My feet carry me over the desert very easily, and for that I'm grateful to you. But I can't go far before I get so hungry and thirsty that I can't stand it.

Lord: What do you want me to do?

Camel: Can you change my body so I can carry enough food and drink with me for many days?

Lord: Yes, I think I can do that.

Narrator 2: Once again the Lord of Heaven reshaped the camel, giving him humps on his back in which to store his food and drink. Camel returned to the desert.

Camel: I've been walking for several days and haven't gotten hungry or thirsty at all. These humps really carry a lot of food and drink.

Narrator 1: But whenever the camel met other animals, they gathered around him and laughed, and laughed, and laughed.

Animal 1: Look at him! He's lumpy and bumpy.

Animal 2: And did you notice his feet? They look like pancakes!

Animal 3: He looks ridiculous.

Camel: Stop making fun of me! Lord of Heaven made me this way.

Animal 1: Then you should go back to Lord of Heaven and ask him to change you.

Narrator 2: The camel's pride was hurt when the animals laughed and teased him. Maybe the Lord of Heaven *could* change him back. So, for the third time, the camel went to the Lord of Heaven.

Lord: Now what? You don't look very happy. I thought you would like what I did to help you.

Camel: I did, for a while. But wherever I go, the other animals stand around me, laugh, and tease me about my humps and bumps and pancake feet. Please, I beg you, change me back to the way I first was.

Lord: I'm afraid that is something that even I can't do. Perhaps if you ignore the other animals, they won't bother you.

Camel: I'll try.

Narrator 1: Camel went away, feeling sad. As he walked, he thought and thought. Then he had a great idea! He turned around and ran back to the Lord of Heaven again.

Camel: I'm sorry to bother you again, but I have one more thing to ask of you. After this, I promise I'll go away and never return.

Lord: Very well. What is it you want this time?

Camel: Give me a superior look! Then I will look down on the other animals and make them think they are inferior to me. After that, they won't laugh at me or tease me.

Lord: You have a clever and excellent idea! I know exactly what to do.

Narrator 2: Lord of Heaven shoved the camel's chin upward. Then he pushed his nose back just a little so that the camel looked as if he smelled something that was unpleasant.

Lord: I think I've done exactly what you asked for. Now go back into the desert and see what happens when you meet other animals.

Narrator 1: The camel returned to the desert, plop-plopping on his large pancake feet. He carried his humps and bumps proudly.

Narrator 2: Soon he met other animals. He sniffed and looked down his nose at them with large and glassy eyes.

Narrator 1: Not one animal laughed or teased him.

Narrator 2: And to this day, all animals and men pull back when they see the proud, superior look of the camel.

Why the Owl Has a Spotted Coat

Summary

Because the owl thinks he's ugly, he never lets his girlfriend see him. One night, while sitting in the shadows of a fire, sparks burn the owl's back. His girlfriend sees him, says she likes him, and they marry. This is a Cherokee tale. RL1

Presentation Suggestions

Both narrators could stand together off to one side. Owl and his girlfriend should be centrally located. Mrs. Owl and the two brothers should be slightly off center.

Props

Since all of the characters are owls, they could wear brown. A small pile of wood could be placed on the stage area to represent the fire.

Delivery

Owl's voice should be a little deep. His girlfriend and Mrs. Owl should have soft, sweet voices. The brothers should have a hint of trickery in their voices.

Related Books

Arnosky, Jim. *All About Owls.* New York: Scholastic, 1995.
McDonald, Megan. *Whoo-oo Is It?* Danbury, CT: Watts, 1992.
Waddell, Martin. *Owl Babies.* Cambridge, MA: Candlewick Press, 1992.

Characters

Narrator 1
Narrator 2
Owl
Girlfriend

Brother 1

Brother 2

Mrs. Owl

Why the Owl Has a Spotted Coat

Narrator 1: Mr. Owl had a girlfriend. He loved her, but she didn't know it.

Narrator 2: Mr. Owl thought he was ugly. When he visited his girlfriend, he'd sit by the dim light of the fire.

Owl: When I sit here, she can't see me. I'm in shadows and darkness.

Girlfriend: Mr. Owl, why don't you come next to me? I want to see how you look.

Owl: I like sitting in the shadows. I can see you and talk to you from here. You don't need to see me.

Narrator 1: Mr. Owl's girlfriend had two brothers. One of their jobs was to bring in firewood for the family. One day, they went into the hills to find wood.

Narrator 2: Now, these brothers liked to play tricks. While they looked for wood, they decided to play a trick on Mr. Owl.

Brother 1: Look what I found, brother. Some wild sumac for the fire!

Brother 2: Sumac doesn't burn well. You should know that. It's bright, but it pops and spatters fire and coals while it's burning.

Brother 1: I know! I think it would be just right for our fire tonight. Just think—Mr. Owl couldn't hide from that.

Brother 2: I get it! Then we'd all see Mr. Owl.

Narrator 1: The brothers brought the wood and the wild sumac home.

Narrator 2: It began to rain, and by the time Mr. Owl arrived, he was very wet.

Mrs. Owl: Boys, start the fire. Mr. Owl is wet and cold. He needs to dry out.

Narrator 1: The brothers started the fire, using the good wood. Mr. Owl sat in the shadows like he always did.

Narrator 2: Soon, the wood burned down.

Brother 1: I'll get some more wood for the fire.

Brother 2: I'll help you.

Narrator 1: When the brothers came back, they had the wild sumac.

Narrator 2: As soon as they put the sumac on the fire, the fire sputtered, sparks flew, and coals were thrown out.

Narrator 1: The sparks burned little spots all over Mr. Owl's back.

Owl: Oh, my! Look at me! Now I have a spotted back! I thought I was ugly before, but now I'm even uglier.

Girlfriend: No you're not, Mr. Owl. I think you look pretty. You're kind and gentle and very smart. What you have on the inside is much more important than how you look on the outside.

Owl: Really? Does that mean you like me?

Girlfriend: Yes. I like you very much.

Owl: Do you like me enough to marry me?

Girlfriend: I thought you'd never ask!

Narrator 1: And so Mr. Owl married his girlfriend. Later, they had children of their own.

Narrator 2: Since then, their children and all owls have spotted coats.

Why Parrots Repeat What People Say

Summary

A farmer who kills his neighbor's water buffalo almost goes to jail because his lorikeet tells what it saw. The farmer creates a plan to make the judge think that the bird lies. The lorikeet is sent to the forest where he meets parrot, another talking bird. Lorikeet advises parrot not to speak his own thoughts. This is a story from Thailand. RL2

Presentation Suggestions

Narrators could be on opposite sides of the stage. The other characters could be across the stage in this order: Neighbor, farmer, lorikeet, parrot. Consider having the judge standing slightly behind the farmer until he is ready to read. Then he could move forward between the farmer and lorikeet until he is finished.

Props

The farmer and neighbor could wear casual clothes. Judge could wear a black robe. Parrot could have some bright feathers pinned on him.

Delivery

Lorikeet should squawk and try to talk like a bird, quick and choppy. Parrot could also sound somewhat like a bird, but without as much squawking. Judge should have an authoritative tone as he reads.

Related Books

Hamsa, Bobbie. *Polly Wants a Cracker.* San Francisco, CA: Children's Press, 1986.
Johnston, Tony. *Lorenzo, the Naughty Parrot.* San Diego, CA: Harcourt, 1992.
Rauzon, Mark J. *Parrots Around the World.* New York: Franklin Watts, 2001.
Zacharias, Thomas. *But Where Is the Green Parrot?* New York: Delacorte, 1968.

Characters

Narrator 1

Narrator 2

Farmer

Neighbor

Lorikeet

Judge

Parrot

Why Parrots Repeat What People Say

Narrator 1: Long, long ago, people did not keep a parrot in the house and teach it to talk. Instead, they had the parrot's cousin, the lorikeet, live in their homes.

Narrator 2: You see, the small lorikeet was smart. It could repeat what it heard and speak its own thoughts. But one day, all that changed, as you are about to hear.

Farmer: What do I see in my rice field? It looks like my neighbor's water buffalo. I've told him time and time again to keep his buffalo on his own land. I will teach my neighbor a lesson.

Narrator 1: The farmer took his neighbor's buffalo, killed it, and cut up the meat. He cooked some of it to eat and hid the rest of it.

Farmer: I'll hide some of the meat on top of my rice house, and I'll hide some of it in my rice bin. No one will *ever* find the meat.

Narrator 2: Now, this farmer had a wonderful lorikeet in his house. The lorikeet saw what the farmer did, and he knew where the farmer hid the meat.

Narrator 1: The next day, the neighbor came to the farmer's house.

Neighbor: I'm looking for my water buffalo. It may be lost. Have you seen it?

Farmer: No, I haven't seen a lost buffalo. I don't know where he might be.

Narrator 2: But the lorikeet knew, and it called out.

Lorikeet: *Awwwk!* My master killed it. *Awwwk!* My master ate some. *Awwwk!* My master hid the rest in the rice bins. *Awwwk!*

Neighbor: What's this? Your lorikeet says you hid parts of my buffalo in your rice bins.

Farmer: Don't believe my lorikeet. He doesn't always tell the truth. Why would I do such a thing to your buffalo?

Neighbor: If you don't mind, I'll look in your rice bins and see for myself.

Narrator 1: The neighbor looked where the lorikeet had said and found the meat.

Neighbor: There is the meat! Your lorikeet told the truth.

Farmer: This is where I always keep meat. But this is the meat of another animal. I did not see your buffalo.

Lorikeet: *Awwwk!* He killed it. *Awwwk!* He ate some. *Awwwk!* Part he hid in the rice bin and part he hid over the rice house. *Awwwk!* This is your buffalo.

Farmer: Don't listen to him. The bird is not telling the truth.

Narrator 2: The neighbor was confused. Should he believe the farmer or the lorikeet?

Neighbor: Meet me in court tomorrow. We'll let the judge settle this matter.

Narrator 1: The farmer knew he would have to come up with a plan so he wouldn't go to jail. That night, he put the lorikeet's cage in a big brass pot. He covered the pot with a cloth so that it was dark inside. Outside, the moon was full, and the night was clear and bright. But the lorikeet could not see this.

Narrator 2: The farmer beat on the pot for a long time. First he beat softly. Then a little louder. Then he beat the pot so loudly that it sounded like thunder.

Narrator 1: The farmer wet a cloth with water and let it drip on the pot so that it sounded like rain.

Narrator 2: All night long, the farmer pounded and dripped the water. He stopped just before the sun came up. He removed the cage from the pot and took off the cover.

Farmer: Now, my little friend, it's time for us to get ready to go to court. The judge will be waiting for us.

Judge: We are here today to find out what happened to this man's water buffalo. Tell me what you know.

Neighbor: Well, sir, I lost my water buffalo and went to look for it. When I reached my neighbor's house, his lorikeet told me where to look. I found the meat where the lorikeet said it would be.

Judge: Lorikeet, tell me what you said.

Lorikeet: *Awwwk!* Master stole it. *Awwwk!* Master killed it! *Awwwk!* Master ate part. Hid the rest in the rice bins.

Judge: It sounds like the farmer is guilty. Take him to jail!

Farmer: Wait! The meat that was in the rice bins was from another animal. How can you believe a bird and not me?

Judge: I believe the lorikeet. He is a smart bird.

Farmer: This is true. He is smart, but he loves to lie. Ask my lorikeet something else. Ask him what kind of a night we had last night.

Judge: Very well. Lorikeet, tell me, what kind of night did we have last night?

Lorikeet: *Awwwk!* Terrible night. *Awwwk!* Dark and stormy. *Awwwk!* Wind blew. Rained hard. *Awwwk!* Thunder roared. Scary night!

Farmer: If you remember, Judge, last night was calm and clear. The moon was full and bright. You see, the bird loves to tell stories.

Judge: I can see that. You are free to go home. Think about this, though. Your bird put your life in danger. From now on, no one should keep a lorikeet in his house. Even though the bird is smart, we should not care for him as though he were one of us.

Narrator 1: The farmer went home a free man. He opened the cage door and told his lorikeet to go away.

Farmer: Go on! Fly away! I don't ever want to see you in my house again!

Narrator 2: The lorikeet flew into the forest and learned to find his own food and take care of himself. One day, he met a beautiful bird. It was larger than he was. It had bright red and green feathers.

Lorikeet: *Awwwk!* I've never seen you before. Who are you?

Parrot: I am the parrot, and I have come from the south. Now I am going to live here. *Ark!* I can talk the language of man.

Lorikeet: *Awwwk!* Welcome! Since you are a stranger here, let me give you some advice. *Awwwk!* I can speak the language of man, too. I lived in man's house many years. *Awwwk!* He took care of me.

Narrator 1: The lorikeet told his story to the parrot, and how telling the truth got him in trouble.

Lorikeet: Let me warn you. *Awwwk!* When man learns that you can speak his language, he will bring you into his house. *Awwwk!* He will teach you what to say. Repeat his words and nothing more. *Awwwk!* Do not speak your own mind. *Awwwk!* Man loves to hear his own thoughts.

Parrot: Thank you. I'll remember what you've told me. *Ark!*

Narrator 2: Sure enough, the lorikeet was right. Man learned that there was a talking parrot. He caught it and brought it to his house where he fed and cared for it.

Narrator 1: Man taught him things to say. Parrot remembered what lorikeet had told him.

Narrator 2: He was afraid to say his true thoughts. So, to this day, a parrot never says what it thinks. It just repeats what people say.

Why the Redbird Is Red

Summary

Because a bird pecks mud out of a wolf's eyes, the wolf wants to pay the bird to show his appreciation. Using red clay with oil, the wolf gives the bird a colorful new coat. This is a Cherokee tale. RL2

Presentation Suggestions

Narrators could stand on opposite sides of the stage. The redbirds and wolf should stand in the center of the stage.

Props

The two birds should wear brown. Perhaps, when Mr. Redbird is painted red, the reader could remove his/her brown shirt, revealing a red one underneath.

Delivery

The wolf's voice should be deeper than the birds' voices. Both birds should have high-pitched voices, with Mrs. Redbird's voice a little higher than Mr. Redbird's.

Related Books

Maloney, Peter, and Felicia Zekauskas. *Redbird at Rockefeller Center.* New York: Dial Books, 1997.
Preller, James. *Cardinal and Sunflower.* New York: HarperCollins, 1998.
Stone, Lynn. *Cardinals—Backyard Birds.* Vero Beach, FL: Rourke Book Co., 1998.

Characters

Narrator 1
Narrator 2
Mr. Redbird
Wolf
Mrs. Redbird

Why the Redbird Is Red

Narrator 1: Long ago, the redbirds were only brown. They didn't have any color at all.

Narrator 2: Mr. Redbird was a hard worker. Every morning he went to find food for his family.

Narrator 1: He would look for nuts, berries, and worms. After he fed his family, he'd go out to find food for himself.

Narrator 2: One morning, while he was looking for his food, he heard sobs from behind a rock.

Mr. Redbird: What could that noise be? It sounds like someone is hurt.

Narrator 1: Redbird looked behind the rock and saw a wolf.

Mr. Redbird: You sound bad. What happened?

Wolf: You won't believe me when I tell you.

Mr. Redbird: Sure I will. Try me.

Wolf: This morning I saw a raccoon in the woods. We talked for a while and then he said mean things to me.

Mr. Redbird: That wasn't nice of him. What did you do?

Wolf: I chased him up into a tree that hung out over the river.

Mr. Redbird: Did you follow him?

Wolf: No. I saw the raccoon in the river, but I didn't know it was just his reflection. I jumped into the water to get it and almost drowned.

Mr. Redbird: I'm glad you didn't drown. That must have been scary.

Wolf: It was. When I pulled myself out of the river, I was tired. I fell asleep on the riverbank.

Mr. Redbird: That's good.

Wolf: Not really. While I was sleeping, the raccoon packed mud over my eyes. I couldn't see. In fact, I still can't see very well. Look at my eyes—are they still covered with mud?

Mr. Redbird: Yes they are. Let me see if I can help get the mud out of your eyes.

Narrator 2: The redbird pecked mud from the wolf's eyes. He took out most of the mud, but there was still a little bit left.

Mr. Redbird: How does that feel?

Wolf: My eyes are sore, but they feel much better now.

Mr. Redbird: Come to the river with me and I'll wash your face. That will get the rest of the mud out.

Narrator 1: The wolf was happy that the redbird could help him.

Wolf: I would like to pay you for your kindness. What would you like?

Mr. Redbird: I really can't think of anything.

Wolf: How would you like to have a new colorful coat?

Mr. Redbird: I think that would be nice. What color do you have in mind?

Wolf: Red! See that rock over there?

Narrator 2: Wolf pointed to a big broken rock. It had red clay and oil inside.

Wolf: That red clay will make a fine paint for you.

Narrator 1: Wolf painted the bird and was pleased with his work.

Narrator 2: The bird was pleased, too. He couldn't wait to get home to show his wife.

Mrs. Redbird: You look beautiful! Where did you get such a lovely color? Who did this to you?

Narrator 1: The bird told her what had happened.

Mr. Redbird: The red clay with oil made the best paint.

Mrs. Redbird: Tell me where the rock is. I want to be red too.

Narrator 2: Mr. Redbird told her where to find the rock. She went there and took some paint. She quickly painted herself, and then rushed home where Mr. Redbird was minding the babies.

Mr. Redbird: You look very nice, but why didn't you put on more red paint? You're not as bright as I am.

Mrs. Redbird: I was in a hurry. I wanted to return to my children.

Narrator 1: And ever since then, all male redbirds are bright red because of Mr. Redbird's kindness to the wolf.

Narrator 2: But because Mrs. Redbird was in a hurry, female redbirds have only a little bit of red.

Why the Woodpecker Looks for Bugs

Summary

The Great One visits a mean old woman and entrusts her with his bag. In spite of his warning not to open the bag, she does, and immediately the bugs that were inside his bag escape. Angry that the old woman had disobeyed him, The Great One uses his powers and turns her into a woodpecker. This is a Native American tale. RL2

Presentation Suggestions

The narrators could stand together to the front and side of the stage, while the old woman and the Great One could stand near each other slightly off center.

Props

The Great One could hold a brown grocery bag, which he would later hand over to the old woman. If possible, the old woman could wear a red wig.

Delivery

The old woman could speak in a raspy, high-pitched, and slightly whiny voice. The Great One's voice should be deep and smooth.

Related Books

Hurd, Edith Thatcher. *Look for a Bird*. New York: HarperCollins, 1997.
Stone, Lynn. *Woodpeckers—Backyard Birds*. Vero Beach, FL: Rourke Book Co., 1998.
Tejima, Keizaburo. *Woodpecker Forest*. New York: Putnam, 1989.
Wildsmith, Brian. *The Owl and the Woodpecker*. Danbury, CT: Franklin Watts, Inc., 1977.

Characters

Narrator 1
Narrator 2
Old Woman
Great One

Why the Woodpecker Looks for Bugs

Narrator 1: Long, long ago, there was an old woman who lived alone. She had a very long nose and bright red hair.

Narrator 2: She was not a kind woman, or even a good woman. In fact, many people did not like her.

Narrator 1: This woman was also very nosey. She always wanted to know where everyone went, what they did, and why they did it.

Old Woman: Hmmm, I see the lady across the street has a new friend. I'll have to find out who she is, where she came from, and why she came here.

Narrator 2: Yes, she always had to know everything about everyone.

Narrator 1: One day, the Great One, who had magical powers, decided to visit her.

Great One: I hear so many bad things about the old woman. I must see for myself if she has any good in her at all.

Narrator 2: As the Great One was walking down the road to her home, the old woman was walking up the road. They met in the middle of the road. The old woman didn't know who he was.

Old Woman: Hello. You're new in town, aren't you? I've never seen you before.

Great One: I've never been here before. I'm just passing through.

Old Woman: Where did you come from? Where are you going?

Great One: No place special. But I've been walking for a long time, and as you can see, I have this big bag with me. I would like to walk around the town, but I don't want to carry the bag.

Old Woman: I'll take your bag home with me and keep it for you while you walk around town.

Great One: Thank you. That's very nice of you. All I ask is that you do not open the bag. Not for any reason. Do you understand?

Old Woman: Of course. I'll do as you say and not open your bag.

Narrator 1: The Great One went on his way and was soon out of sight.

Old Woman: I wonder what's in this bag. I'll take a little peek and see. Then I'll close the bag and no one will ever know that I looked into it.

Narrator 2: The old woman opened the bag. Right away, bugs came out and ran all over the place. Bugs ran up the road. Bugs ran down the road. Bugs crawled up her body.

Narrator 1: The old woman didn't know what to do.

Old Woman: I wish I had never opened the bag! Now I have to catch the bugs and put them back into it or the man will know I opened his bag.

Narrator 2: She ran after the bugs, trying to pick them up and put them back into the bag. But it was hopeless.

Narrator 1: The sun went down and it began to get dark. The old woman was tired of chasing bugs and went home.

Narrator 2: When she reached her home, the Great One was waiting for her.

Great One: Where is my bag?

Old Woman: I . . . I . . . it . . . it . . .

Great One: You opened it, didn't you? Where are my bugs?

Narrator 1: The old woman told him what she had done.

Old Woman: Your bugs are in the grass, in the road, in the trees. I tried to get all of them, but I couldn't. They're everywhere. I know I shouldn't have opened your bag, and I'm sorry.

Narrator 2: The Great One stood tall. He pointed at the old woman.

Great One: Woman is supposed to be nice. Woman is supposed to be helpful. Woman is supposed to be honest. You are none of these. You are not fit to be a woman.

Narrator 1: As he spoke, the old woman began to shrink. She got smaller and smaller.

Narrator 2: Feathers covered her body. Her arms disappeared and were replaced with wings. The Great One had turned her into a woodpecker.

Narrator 1: She flew through the open window and began picking up bugs.

Narrator 2: Today, woodpeckers are still trying to find all the bugs that got out of the big bag.

How the Bluebird Became Blue

Summary

Creator made all birds look alike so they could choose their own color. One bird wanted to be blue, like the sky. He followed Creator's directions and got his wish. This is a Native American (Seneca) tale. RL2

Presentation Suggestions

The narrators could be separated. Creator should be in the center, with the birds clustered around him. Bluebird should be closest to Creator. Consider having the other birds step forward to read their parts and then move to the side of the stage when finished.

Props

All of the birds should wear brown. Creator should wear white or a neutral color. Perhaps the bluebird could slip on a blue shirt when he notices he has become blue.

Delivery

Creator should have a smooth, warm voice. The birds should have higher pitched voices, with a variety of inflections, intonations, and volume levels.

Related Books

Friskey, Margaret. *Birds We Know.* Danbury, CT: Children's Press, 1981.
Margolis, Richard J. *Big Bear, Spare That Tree.* New York: Greenwillow, 1980.
Newton, Patricia Montgomery. *The Frog Who Drank the Waters of the World.* New York: Atheneum, 1982.
Oppenheim, Joanne. *Have You Seen Birds?* New York: Scholastic, 1986.

Characters

Narrator 1
Narrator 2
Creator

Bird 1

Bird 2

Bird 3

Bird 4

Bluebird

How the Bluebird Became Blue

Narrator 1: When Creator made the world, he filled it with many beautiful colors.

Narrator 2: Except for the birds. He made them all the same color.

Creator: I think they should find the colors they like best. That way, they'll be happy with the way they look.

Narrator 1: The birds were easily mixed up because they all looked the same.

Narrator 2: They were always fighting.

Bird 1: Who are you? You look like me and like all the other birds around here.

Bird 2: No I don't. If you look closely, you'll see I don't look anything like you. You don't know what to look for.

Bird 3: I think he's right. Look around you. We all look the same.

Bird 4: Hah! That's what you think. I look much nicer than you do.

Narrator 1: The birds always picked on each other. It was terrible!

Narrator 2: One spring day, one of the birds looked up at the bright blue sky.

Bluebird: I can't remember ever seeing the sky so blue. It's a beautiful color of blue! Oh, how I wish that my coat looked like that.

Narrator 1: Creator heard the bird.

Creator: Would you like to be blue like the sky?

Bluebird: Oh, yes! I'd give anything to be that color.

Creator: What would you give to me if I made you blue?

Bluebird: I would give you all my thanks and I would try to please you always.

Creator: Very well. Then do as I say. For the next four mornings, when you dip in the lake for your bath, fly back to this branch and sing, "I am glad I am going to be like the sky."

Bluebird: I'll do as you say. I'll go to the lake right away.

Narrator 2: When the bird reached the lake, he looked into it.

Bluebird: The lake is as blue as the sky! I'm sure that when I dip into it, my feathers will become wet with blue.

Narrator 1: The bird dipped into the lake, then flew to the branch of the tree. He sat in the sun and waited for his feathers to turn blue. But nothing happened.

Bluebird: My feathers are still brown. I'll sing the song Creator told me to sing. Maybe that will help.

Narrator 2: Singing the song didn't work.

Bluebird: Well, Creator did tell me to dip into the lake four times. This was only the first. I have to do it three more times.

Narrator 1: The bird dipped in the lake, flew back to the branch, and sang the song two more times.

Narrator 2: On the fourth morning, while he was singing his song on the branch, he heard Creator's voice.

Creator: You have followed my directions well, little bird. Are you sure that you want to be the same color as the sky?

Bluebird: I do, I do! I still think that is the most beautiful color I've ever seen, and I want to look just like the sky.

Creator: Then here's what you must do. Go to the lake and dip in the water one more time. Make sure that you touch nothing at all but the water.

Bluebird: I'll do that.

Creator: Wait, there's more. After you have dipped, then fly upward and sing, "I have been touched by the brush that colored the sky."

Bluebird: I'll go right away and do what you said.

Narrator 1: The bird dove deep into the lake to make sure that his body was covered with the water. When he came to the top, he was out of breath and too tired to fly.

Narrator 2: He walked slowly through the water to the shore. His breast rubbed across the red clay of the bank.

Bluebird: That was harder than I thought it would be. I must rest before I fly upward.

Narrator 1: Soon he was rested and able to fly. The air dried his feathers.

Narrator 2: As he waved his wings, he noticed that they were now the color of the sky. He was overjoyed and sang the song Creator had taught him.

Bluebird: I have been touched by the brush that colored the sky! Creator has made me beautiful! Thank you, thank you, Creator. You gave me what I wanted.

Creator: You are welcome, little bird. And I notice that your breast is red from touching the clay when you came out of the water. This is good. Now you have the magic of the sky on your wings and a touch of earth on your breast. In you, the skyworld and the earthworld meet. I must say, you are very beautiful. I think Bluebird would be a good name for you.

Narrator 1: And now you know the story of the first bluebird.

Narrator 2: Since then, bluebirds sing a sweet song of thanks to Creator. Listen for it!

Why Robin Has a Red Breast

Summary

Robin runs out of the red camwood powder he and his wife use when they dress up. He discovers that only one trader in town has a small amount in stock. As the robin carries it home in his beak, it melts and dribbles down his chest, coloring it red. This is a tale from the African Congo. RL3

Presentation Suggestions

The narrators could stand together off to one side. The two robins should be centrally located, and the four traders could be grouped on the other side of the stage area.

Props

The robins could wear brown, and at the end, perhaps the male robin could cover his chest with red felt or paper that has velcro or double-sided tape on it.

Delivery

Each trader should develop a specific vocal style that differs from each other. One could be deep, one could have a drawl, one could speak in a fast pace, and so forth. The female robin's voice should be a little higher pitched than the male's voice.

Related Books

Klevin, Elisa. *The Lion and the Little Red Bird.* New York: Dutton, 1992.
Robinson, Fay. *Singing Robins.* Minneapolis, MN: Lerner Publications, 2000.
Wood, A. J. *Beautiful Birds.* Honesdale, PA: Boyds Mills Press, 1991.

Characters

Narrator 1

Narrator 2

Robin

Wife

Trader 1

Trader 2
Trader 3
Trader 4

Why Robin Has a Red Breast

Narrator 1: One day, Robin and his little wife were getting dressed up and realized that they were out of camwood powder.

Narrator 2: They always used this red powder from a special tree when they wanted to look pretty.

Robin: How could we be out of camwood powder so soon? I just got some a few days ago.

Wife: Well, we have been getting dressed up a lot lately. We weren't paying attention to how much we were using. You'll just have to get more.

Robin: Very well. I'll go to town and buy some.

Narrator 1: Robin went to the first trader he came to at the market.

Robin: I need to buy some camwood powder. My wife and I use it often, so I think I should buy a big supply.

Trader 1: Sorry, Mr. Robin. I'm out of camwood powder and don't have any in stock. Maybe another trader will be able to help you.

Narrator 2: Robin went to a second trader.

Robin: I'm looking for camwood powder. Do you have any?

Trader 2: Nope! Don't have any at all. It sure is popular. I've been selling a lot of it these days. Sorry I can't help you.

Narrator 1: Robin went to a third trader.

Trader 3: May I help you?

Robin: I sure hope so. I'm looking for camwood powder and can't find it anywhere. Do you have some?

Trader 3: I just sold my last powder a couple of days ago. Guess I can't help you after all.

Narrator 2: Robin went from trader to trader, but everyone was all sold out of camwood powder.

Narrator 1: There was only one trader left in the town. Robin hoped that this one might have the red powder he sought.

Narrator 2: He didn't want to have to return home without the powder. He knew his wife would be disappointed if he did. Robin went into the last shop.

Robin: I'm looking for camwood powder. Do you have any?

Trader 4: Let me look in the back room.

Narrator 1: The trader soon returned.

Trader 4: Here is a little bit. It's not enough for me to sell, but it might be enough for you to use for yourself. You can have it.

Robin: Thank you very much. It's better than not having any. Now I must take this home to my wife.

Narrator 2: Robin put the little bit of camwood powder in his mouth and headed home.

Narrator 1: The red camwood powder began to melt in his mouth. It became a runny paste, and as he flew, it dribbled out.

Robin: Oh dear, I'm losing the powder. I'll close my beak tighter. Maybe that will stop the powder from running out of my mouth.

Narrator 2: But no matter how tight he held his beak, the red paste made streaks around his mouth and dribbled down over his breast.

Narrator 1: By the time he reached home, he didn't have any more red paste in his mouth.

Wife: Look at you! Your breast is all red.

Robin: I know. The small amount of camwood powder I could get melted in my mouth and dribbled onto my breast. I couldn't help it.

Wife: What about me? I want a red breast too!

Narrator 2: But it was not to be. And since that day, the robin has a red breast, while his wife is a drab, brown little bird with no red on her anywhere.

How the Birds Got Their Feathers

Summary

Buzzard makes the long trip to Creator to get clothing for the birds. He's given first choice, with the understanding that he can try on each suit only once. With one suit remaining, he's stuck with it! It's not attractive and doesn't fit. When he returns home and distributes the feathered suits to the birds, he's unhappy and mopes. Then he realizes that if it weren't for him, the birds would have no suits at all. This is an Iroquois tale. RL3

Presentation Suggestions

The narrators could stand together, while the birds remain in the center. You may want to consider having the lesser bird characters step back after reading their lines. Creator could stand off to one side and come forward to stand next to the buzzard when they interact. Consider having Creator return to the side after reading.

Props

The birds should wear neutral colors. Buzzard could pick up a colored paper feather for each suit he tries on. Later, when the narrator tells about the buzzard distributing the feathered suits, he could hand out the colored paper feathers to the birds. Creator should be dressed in white or light colors.

Delivery

Each bird should have a different sounding voice, with a variety of pitches, inflections, tones, pacing, and so on. Buzzard could speak more slowly than the other birds. Creator's voice should be smooth and warm.

Related Books

Bruchac, Joseph. *Iroquois Stories—Heroes and Heroines, Monsters and Magic.* Freedom, CA: Crossing Press, 1985.

Conklin, Gladys. *If I Were a Bird.* New York: Holiday House, 1965.

Kaufmann, John. *Birds Are Flying.* New York: Thomas Y. Crowell, 1979.

Wood, A. J. *Beautiful Birds.* Honesdale, PA: Boyds Mills Press, 1991.

Characters

Narrator 1
Narrator 2
Eagle
Bird 1
Bird 2
Bird 3
Bird 4
Buzzard
Creator

How the Birds Got Their Feathers

Narrator 1: In a time long ago, when animals could talk, birds had no feathers.

Narrator 2: In winter, when it was so cold, they shivered and shook. And in the summer, they felt as though they were being baked.

Narrator 1: Because they had no covering on their bodies, they thought they looked funny, so they hid from sight.

Narrator 2: One day, the eagle had an idea.

Eagle: I'm going to call all the birds together. We must decide what to do about our not having any clothing.

Narrator 1: All the birds near and far came to the eagle's gathering to hear what he had to say.

Eagle: My friends, it is not fair that Creator didn't give our bodies clothing. Other animals are covered—some with fur, some with thick skin, some with shells or scales—but we have nothing. We need to send a messenger to Creator and ask him for covering. Who will go?

Narrator 2: One small bird stepped forward. He looked proud and sure of himself in spite of his size.

Bird 1: I'll be the messenger, and I'll ask Creator for something to cover us.

Narrator 1: Then, the small bird looked up to the sky and was no longer sure if he could do this.

Bird 1: Creator lives far away, doesn't he? I don't know if I could fly that far. In fact, I'm sure I won't be able to make the trip. I'm sorry. I won't be able to go after all.

Narrator 2: The small bird put his head down in shame, and stepped back.

Eagle: Thank you for offering to go little one. Now, who *does* think he'll be able to fly to Creator as our messenger?

Narrator 1: Another bird stepped forward. He was a little bigger than the first one.

Bird 2: Perhaps I could be the messenger and fly to Creator. At least I could try. (*pause*) On second thought, that is far away, and I don't think I could fly that distance. Sorry.

Narrator 2: And the second bird stepped back. One by one, different birds offered to try, but then changed their mind. None of the birds thought they could fly the distance to Creator.

Eagle: There must be one of you who could be our messenger to Creator. Who will it be?

Narrator 1: The birds looked at each other, trying to find one who looked big enough and strong enough to fly so far. Then, one of the birds hopped up and down and pointed to the buzzard.

Bird 3: Look at that buzzard! I bet he could make the trip. Buzzard is big. He has a wide wingspan, and he can fly higher than any of us.

Bird 4: Yes, the buzzard could be our messenger!

Narrator 2: All of the birds went to the buzzard.

Bird 3: Buzzard, will you be our messenger to Creator?

Bird 4: You're the only one who could fly that far, and if you don't go, we won't have any messenger at all.

Buzzard: Huh? You want *me* to fly all the way up there—to the place where Creator lives?

Bird 1: That's right. Please, Buzzard, please.

Buzzard: Well . . . I don't know if I can.

Bird 2: Sure you can, Buzzard. We *know* you can.

Buzzard: I guess I can at least try. (*pause*) Well, okay, I'll do it. But I'll need a few days to get ready.

Narrator 1: For the next three days, the buzzard ate dead field mice, dead rabbits, dead squirrels, and other dead animals that he could find.

Narrator 2: That's all right, though. After all, buzzards always eat dead animals.

Narrator 1: And while the buzzard was eating and getting ready, the other birds made a fire and sent their wishes and prayers on the smoke that went up to Creator.

Narrator 2: Finally, the buzzard announced that he was ready. The other birds watched him lift off from the ground and head for the place where Creator lived.

Narrator 1: It was a long journey, and after a while Buzzard became tired.

Buzzard: I don't think I can go any farther. My wings feel heavy, and I don't know if I can fly any more. But if I don't get to Creator and give him the message, the birds will be very disappointed.

Narrator 2: Just then, a breeze blew gently, and Buzzard caught an air current.

Narrator 1: Buzzard drifted on the air current and was able to rest. Then, when he was no longer tired, he continued his journey.

Narrator 2: He went higher and higher, until he reached the sun.

Buzzard: Whew! It sure is hot here!

Narrator 1: As he passed close to the sun, he felt his head begin to burn.

Buzzard: *Owww!* That hurts!

Narrator 2: The skin on top of his naked head burned red in the sun's heat.

Narrator 1: Buzzard flapped his wings harder and faster, and soon he was away from the sun. Shortly after, he came to the place where Creator lived and landed right in front of Him.

Buzzard: Hi! You must be Creator. I'm Buzzard, and I've come to you from—

Narrator 2: Creator interrupted the buzzard.

Creator: I know why you are here, and I've been waiting for you. The wishes and prayers of the birds reached me long ago. Come with me.

Narrator 1: Creator led Buzzard to a colorful pile of feather clothing that he had prepared.

Creator: Here are beautiful feathered suits for you and your friends.

Narrator 2: The suits were of many colors: red, orange, yellow, green, blue, purple, brown, black, white, and many that had several colors in it.

Buzzard: I've never seen so many beautiful suits!

Creator: Buzzard, I know how hard it was for you to fly to me, so I think it is only fair that you have the first choice.

Buzzard: You mean I can take whichever one I want?

Creator: That's right. However, you may try on each suit only once. If you don't like it, put it aside, but you can't go back to it. And when you find one you like, it's yours.

Buzzard: That's wonderful! I'll choose the finest feathers. Then everyone will see them and always remember that I was the messenger for the birds who brought back their clothing.

Narrator 1: Creator left the buzzard to look for his suit. First, Buzzard tried on a bright blue suit with white feathers and a stylish cap.

Buzzard: Nice suit. Blue is a good color for me. But, it's not bright enough, and besides, it's only the first suit I've tried on. I'm sure to find a better one than this.

Narrator 2: So, he put the blue suit aside, and eventually that was the suit that was given to Blue Jay.

Narrator 1: The next suit he tried on was a brilliant red and black with a tall crest.

Buzzard: This is a little too bright, and I don't look good in red. This won't do.

Narrator 2: He removed the red suit, and that's the one that went to Cardinal.

Narrator 1: Then, Buzzard picked up a brown suit that had a scarlet vest.

Buzzard: This is nice, but vests might not be in style in the future.

Narrator 2: That suit went to Robin. Buzzard tried on suit after suit, but for one reason or another, he put them aside.

Narrator 1: Either the feathers were too long or too short; too shiny or too dull; or the color wasn't right for him.

Narrator 2: Finally, he was down to the last suit. It had dull dirty-brown feathers and looked small. But since there were no more suits, he had no choice but to try it on.

Narrator 1: He pulled, and tugged, and struggled until he finally got it on. It was very, *very* tight.

Narrator 2: He looked down at his legs. They were bare! The suit didn't cover his legs at all!

Narrator 1: His neck was also bare. And what's worse, the red skin of his bald head wasn't covered!

Buzzard: No, this one will *never* do. I'll see if Creator has more suits I can try on. I imagine he has more hidden away somewhere.

Narrator 2: Buzzard went to Creator.

Buzzard: Creator, this was the last suit, and as you can see, it doesn't look very good on me. It doesn't even fit. Do you have any more that I could try on?

Creator: Sorry, Buzzard. That is the only suit left. Now it will have to be yours.

Buzzard: But, Creator, I . . .

Creator: I said, 'No!'

Narrator 1: Buzzard wasn't happy with the decision. He gathered all of the suits and headed home.

Narrator 2: He handed out the suits to the birds. They were delighted with them. As soon as they put them on, the birds flew around showing off their beautiful feathered suits.

Narrator 1: And they sang songs that they'd never sung before. In fact, they're the same songs the birds sing today.

Narrator 2: But Buzzard wasn't happy. He didn't sing. Instead he flew to the top of the tallest tree and moped.

Buzzard: It's not fair. I was the messenger for the birds. If it weren't for me, none of the birds would have their fine clothing.

Narrator 1: Buzzard moped for a long time, then decided to fly around.

Buzzard: All the birds have beautiful suits, but not me. I have the worst one of all. It's just not fair.

Narrator 2: Buzzard made big circles in the sky and flew higher and higher, where he felt close to Creator.

Buzzard: If it weren't for me . . . Yeah! That's right! If it weren't for *me,* the birds wouldn't have their fine suits. I was the one chosen to be the messenger for all the birds. And *I* was the one who brought them their suits.

Narrator 1: Even in his tight-fitting suit of dirty feathers and his burned red head, Buzzard began to feel good about himself.

Narrator 2: Today, Buzzard still remembers that he was the only one who could make the long journey to Creator.

Narrator 1: Every now and again, you might see a small, dark dot moving in circles high in the sky. That's probably Buzzard, circling to be near Creator.

Narrator 2: He's proud because he was the one who got the feathered suits for all the birds. And that's how the birds got their feathers.

Why Owl Hides During the Day

Summary

In the beginning, all birds looked the same until the cardinal convinced the Everything-Maker to make each bird look different. The owl constantly criticizes the new appearances, causing the Everything-Maker to take revenge on him. This is an Iroquois tale. RL5

Presentation Suggestions

The narrators could be on opposite sides of the stage area. The cardinal and the Everything-Maker should be centered. The other birds could be grouped on one side of the stage. Each could step forward when ready to read.

Props

Characters could wear colors that depict the bird they represent. The Everything-Maker should wear a neutral color. Consider having the birds wear signs around their necks to help identify them.

Delivery

Each bird should have its own voice, varying the pitch and volume level to be distinct.

Related Books

Arnosky, Jim. *All About Owls.* New York: Scholastic, 1995.
Lobel, Arnold. *Owl at Home.* New York: HarperCollins, 1975.
Stone, Lynn. *Owls.* Vero Beach, FL: The Rourke Book Co., 1989.

Characters

Narrator 1
Narrator 2
Cardinal
Everything-Maker
Swan
Egret

Cedar Waxwing
Owl
Hummingbird
Phoebe

Why Owl Hides During the Day

Narrator 1: In the beginning, the Everything-Maker made all the birds the same.

Narrator 2: They all had the same strong wings. Their beaks were the same size. And they all had beautiful brown feathers.

Narrator 1: One day, the cardinal noticed something and went to see the Everything-Maker.

Cardinal: How come all of the birds look the same, while other things you made look different?

Everything-Maker: What things are different?

Cardinal: Like the flowers—you made them different shapes and colors.

Everything-Maker: I know. Having them look the same was boring.

Cardinal: And look what you did when you made the animals! You made them all sizes and shapes. And they have different kinds of eyes, ears, noses, and tails. You even gave them different kinds of clothing.

Everything-Maker: True, true, true. Since I made so many animals, I thought we needed several kinds. Anything else?

Cardinal: Yes, the trees. You made some trees short and some tall, and they all have different leaves.

Everything-Maker: What are you trying to say, Cardinal?

Cardinal: Instead of the birds looking alike, why can't we look different from each other? Do you think you could help us?

Everything-Maker: Sure I can. Bring all the birds to me and I'll see what they'd like me to do.

Narrator 2: Cardinal went to all the birds and gave them the message.

Cardinal: Go to the Everything-Maker. He's going to make us all different!

Narrator 1: The birds flew to the Everything-Maker.

Everything-Maker: Now, my bird friends, I know you all want to look different from each other. Tell me what you want me to do.

Cardinal: Since I came to you with the idea, I'd like to go first. I love the color red, and would like to be all red.

Everything-Maker: And so you will.

Narrator 2: Cardinal's brown feathers turned red right away.

Cardinal: Look at me, everyone! I'm beautiful! Thank you!

Everything-Maker: Who's next?

Swan: Me! I've always wanted to look lovely. Would you make me pure white, with a long, curving neck?

Everything-Maker: That's easy.

Narrator 1: Faster than you could wink an eye, Swan reached out her long neck. She looked behind her and saw that she was all white.

Swan: That's just what I wanted, Everything-Maker! I'm grateful to you.

Egret: Oh, sir, make me white like Swan! And give me long legs and a beak that is long and sharp like a spear so I can catch fish.

Narrator 2: Again, the Everything-Maker made the change, and Egret was delighted.

Narrator 1: One by one the birds told the Everything-Maker how they wanted to look. Some asked for beautiful colored feathers, while others wanted their legs or beaks changed.

Narrator 2: The Everything-Maker listened carefully to each wish and made the change. Every bird was happy.

Narrator 1: As Everything-Maker made the changes, Owl looked down from a branch above the Everything-Maker. While Owl watched and waited for his turn, he made mean remarks.

Cedar Waxwing: I think it would be fun to have a mask over my eyes.

Owl: Are you hiding from something? Don't you want to be recognized?

Hummingbird: I'd like to have green feathers and a red throat. I like those colors best.

Owl: Ugh! That's much too flashy!

Phoebe: I think a carefree, wind-blown look to the feathers around my head would be good for me.

Everything-Maker: I'll fluff up your feathers a bit, which should give you the look you want.

Owl: Phoebe, your feathers are sure messed up! Do you need a comb?

Narrator 2: Owl's comments were not at all nice, and the Everything-Maker was angry.

Everything-Maker: That's enough out of you, Owl. If you can't say something nice, then be quiet and don't say anything at all.

Owl: I can't help it! I'm just remarking about what I see. And what I see is dumb looking, stupid, or silly. I don't know why the birds want such looks.

Everything-Maker: If you don't like what you see, then don't look!

Narrator 1: Owl didn't pay any attention to the Everything-Maker, and continued to make remarks as the birds changed their looks.

Owl: All of you birds are making it easy for me. I'm going to be the most beautiful of all of you. I'll be handsome, and I'll be fast. I'm not going to ask for any of the stupid things you are.

Narrator 2: The Everything-Maker couldn't take it any more. He grabbed Owl and pushed his head into his body.

Narrator 1: Then he held Owl by the ears and shook him long and hard, until Owl's eyes opened wide and became very round.

Owl: Oh, the sun hurts my eyes!

Everything-Maker: That's because they're so wide. From now on, you'll be better off getting out of the sun and sleeping during the day. Then at night, when it's dark, you can be awake. And since you don't have much of a neck any more, you won't be able to watch what you're not supposed to.

Narrator 2: Then the Everything-Maker threw a handful of mud at Owl, making him all brown.

Owl: Brown! I don't want to be such a dull color! I want to be beautiful and handsome.

Everything-Maker: Sorry, Owl. Now, go away and let me finish my work with the birds.

Narrator 1: Owl was bothered by the way he looked and went back to his nest to get away from everyone.

Narrator 2: Since then, Owl sleeps during the day and is awake at night.

Why Flies Buzz

Summary

When a man drops his knife from the top of a palm tree, it triggers a chain of events that eventually leads to the bush-fowl neglecting to wake the sun. Great Spirit investigates and finds that the source of the trouble is a black fly. This is a tale from Eastern Nigeria, Africa. RL 2

Presentation Suggestions

The narrators could be off to one side, with the husband and wife close to them. Consider having the animals seated in a second row, coming forward to read their lines, then returning to their position. When the Great Spirit is introduced, he could walk to the center. The animals could again come forward to read when the Great Spirit talks to each one, and return when they finish reading.

Props

If desired, symbolic colors or characteristics could be used for the characters—big ears for the elephant, long tail for the monkey, and so forth. The husband could hold a plastic knife and drop it at the appropriate time.

Delivery

Each character should develop a voice that might reflect the animal or person portrayed. Experiment with different vocal ranges, pacing, volume levels, and maybe even a dialect or accent.

Related Books

Aylesworth, Jim. *Old Black Fly.* New York: Henry Holt & Co., 1992.
Conklin, Gladys. *I Watch Flies.* New York: Holiday House, 1977.
Elkin, Benjamin. *Why the Sun Was Late.* Berkeley, CA: Parent's Press, 1966.
McClintock, Marshall. *A Fly Went By.* New York: Random House, 1958.

Characters

Narrator 1
Narrator 2

Husband
Wife
Snake
Rat
Bird
Monkey
Elephant
Bush-fowl
Great Spirit
Ant Heap
Flowering Creeper
Mango
Knife
Black Fly

Why Flies Buzz

Narrator 1: One day, a man and his wife were collecting nuts in the bush. The man saw clusters of ripe nuts at the top of a palm tree. He told his wife to wait below while he climbed the tree, carrying his knife in his belt.

Narrator 2: While he hacked away at the palm nuts, a small black fly buzzed around his face, tickling his nose while trying to get to the corner of the man's eye.

Husband: Go away, fly. Quit bothering me.

Narrator 1: As he brushed the fly away, his knife fell from his hand.

Husband: Wife! Get out of the way! The knife is falling.

Narrator 2: His wife jumped to one side and the knife missed her.

Wife: That was a close one, Husband. I'm glad you warned me in time.

Narrator 1: The woman didn't realize that when she got out of the way, she jumped over a snake that was sleeping under the dead leaves.

Snake: What was that? Something big and terrible is trying to get me. I must get away!

Narrator 2: The snake dived into the first hole he came to, which happened to be rat's hole.

Rat: A snake! I *know* he wants to eat me. But he won't if I can get out of here.

Narrator 1: Rat dashed past the snake, out of his hole, and up a tree.

Rat: That was a close call! I should be safe in this tree.

Narrator 2: Rat didn't know that the tree he was in was where the plantain-eater bird had built her nest. The bird thought the rat was after her eggs.

Bird: Squawk! Get away! Get away!

Narrator 1: The bird squawked and screamed so loudly that it scared the monkey just as he was about to eat a nice, juicy mango he had picked. Terrified, the monkey dropped the mango.

Monkey: Whoops! I guess I won't be eating that mango.

Narrator 2: The mango fell with a thud on the back of an elephant who was walking by.

Elephant: Help! Hunters are attacking me.

Narrator 1: He charged off, catching his head in a flowering creeper that was climbing up a tree. He dragged the creeper through the bush as he ran. The creeper's strong stem wrapped around a tall earthen ant heap. It pulled the ant heap to the ground, and it fell on a nest full of bush-fowl's eggs. Every single egg broke! The bush-fowl was *very* angry!

Bush-fowl: *Kark!* Look what you've done to my eggs. They're all broken! Now what will I do?

Narrator 2: The bush-fowl spread her feathers over the ruined nest. She was miserable and didn't say another word for two whole days and nights.

Narrator 1: Now, it is well known that of all the wild creatures, the bush-fowl is always the first one to wake up. And when she wakes up, she makes loud, harsh sounds that wake up the sun. Then the sun rises from his bed and a new day begins.

Narrator 2: But since the bush-fowl was still angry, she didn't call the sun for two days. It was dark, and the other animals wondered why daylight had not come. They called to the Great Spirit of the Heavens.

All Animals: Great Spirit, what happened?

Great Spirit: I don't know, but I will find out. I want everyone to come to me right away.

Narrator 1: They all came, including the bush-fowl.

Great Spirit: Bush-fowl, why didn't you wake the sun these last two mornings?

Bush-fowl: The ant heap fell on my eggs and broke them. I was too angry to wake the sun.

Great Spirit: Ant heap, why were you so careless that you fell on the bush-fowl's eggs and broke them?

Ant Heap: It wasn't my fault. I was pulled over by the flowering creeper.

Great Spirit: Creeper, why did you pull over the ant heap? It sounds as though you were not careful.

Creeper: I couldn't help it! The elephant dragged me down.

Great Spirit: All right, Elephant. Why did you pull down the flowering creeper?

Elephant: A mango fell on my back and I thought hunters were attacking me.

Great Spirit: Mango, what do you have to say for yourself? Why did you fall on Elephant's back and frighten him?

Mango: Monkey dropped me from a high branch in the tree. Elephant was in the way, and I couldn't stop myself from hitting him.

Great Spirit: Dropping the mango was careless of you, Monkey. Look how frightened you made Elephant.

Monkey: I was frightened, too! A bird was squawking and making such a terrible noise that I thought danger was coming.

Great Spirit: What terrible danger were you squawking about, Bird?

Bird: There was no danger to the animals, but a rat was in my tree, and I thought it was after my eggs. That's why I made so much noise.

Great Spirit: Is this true, Rat? Were you after the plantain-eating bird's eggs?

Rat: No. Oh, no! A snake came into my hole and scared me. I was sure he was going to eat me.

Great Spirit: Now it's your turn, Snake. Why did you go into Rat's hole?

Snake: I was sleeping under some dead leaves, and a man's wife woke me up. She scared me and I dove into the nearest hole I could find.

Great Spirit: Wife, why did you wake Snake? You gave him quite a scare.

Wife: I didn't know Snake was under the leaves. I just jumped out of the way of a knife that fell toward me.

Great Spirit: Interesting. Now Knife, why did you make the woman jump and run?

Knife: Her husband dropped me.

Great Spirit: Husband, knives are dangerous tools, and dropping one could hurt someone. Why did you drop the knife?

Husband: I was cutting palm nuts and trying to brush away a black fly that was tickling me.

Great Spirit: Ah ha! It seems to me that a black fly is the cause of all this trouble. So, I ask you, Black Fly, why did you bother and tickle the man's face while he was up in the palm tree?

Narrator 2: Instead of answering nicely as the others had done, the black fly flew around their heads, saying only one thing.

Black Fly: Buzz! Buzz! Buzz!

Great Spirit: Don't ignore me! I'll ask you again. Why did you tickle the man's face while he was in the tree?

Black Fly: Buzz! Buzz! Buzz!

Great Spirit: You're making me mad, Fly! Since you won't answer my question, I will take away your power of speech. Since you like to say "Buzz" so much, that is what you'll say from this day on. And you, Bush-fowl, must never again forget to call the sun at dawn no matter what happens to your eggs.

Bush-Fowl: I'm sorry. I promise I'll never forget again.

Narrator 1: Bush-fowl kept her promise and always called the sun at dawn.

Narrator 2: And Black Fly never got back his voice, so to this day, Black Fly and his brothers fly all over the world saying, "Buzz! Buzz! Buzz!"

How the Bee Got His Bumble

Summary

Bee discovers that man is the sweetest creature in the world and returns to tell Delbegen. This seven-headed giant plans to eat only this sweet creature. To prevent this from happening, Sartak-Pai, a brave man, removes the bee's tongue so he can't talk. This is a tale from southern Siberia. RL3

Presentation Suggestions

The narrators could be on opposite sides of the stage area. Delbegen should be centered, followed by bee, dog, cat, man, and Sartak-Pai. Perhaps bee could move from one character to another as he interacts with them.

Props

Consider having dog, cat, and bee dressed in appropriate colors. Dog and cat could wear symbolic tails and/or ears.

Delivery

Delbegen's voice should be deep to depict his size. Dog, cat, and bee should vary their voices and try to imitate the animal they represent.

Related Books

Barton, Byron. *Buzz, Buzz, Buzz.* New York: Macmillan, 1973.
Brown, Margaret Wise. *Bumble Bee.* New York: HarperCollins, 1999.
Flanagan, Alice K. *Learning About Bees from Mr. Krebs.* New York: Children's Press, 1999.
Wong, Janet S. *Buzz.* San Diego, CA: Harcourt, 2000.

Characters

Narrator 1
Narrator 2
Delbegen
Bee

Dog
Cat
Man
Sartak-Pai

How the Bee Got His Bumble

Narrator 1: Once there was a giant who had seven heads. His name was Delbegen.

Narrator 2: Because he had seven heads, Delbegen also had seven mouths. He was always looking for something good to eat so he could fill his huge stomach.

Delbegen: This rabbit looks tasty.

Narrator 1: And he popped the rabbit into one of his mouths.

Delbegen: This little mouse is just the right size for a snack.

Narrator 2: He picked up the mouse by its tail and gulped it down.

Delbegen: That was not as good as I thought it would be. Finding food that's sweet is hard when one has so many mouths. There must be an easy way to discover sweet flesh without having to test each one.

Narrator 1: Just then, Delbegen saw a little bee flying around from place to place. The bee would land on something, stay for less than a minute, then fly off again.

Delbegen: That bee is a busy fellow, and he sure does get around. I bet he could be of service to me.

Narrator 2: Delbegen put out his forefinger and beckoned to the bee.

Delbegen: Come here, little bee, I have a job for you.

Bee: What sort of job?

Delbegen: I notice how you fly to so many things, land, and then fly away again. I'm looking for sweet flesh, and I think you can help me find it.

Bee: How do you think I can do that?

Delbegen: Go to every creature on earth and bite each one. Then, return to me and tell me which one is the sweetest. The one you choose will be the one I'll always eat, and I won't bother any other creature.

Bee: I can do that! But it might take me a while to bite every creature, so be patient.

Narrator 1: Bee flew off until he came to a dog. He landed on the dog and bit him.

Dog: Ouch! That hurt! Why did you bite me?

Bee: I'm looking for the sweetest creature for Delbegen, the seven-headed giant. But I didn't like the way you tasted.

Narrator 2: Bee left the dog and soon came to a cat. He bit the cat.

Cat: *Yeow!* Why did you bite me, Bee?

Bee: I wanted to see if you were sweet, but you're not, so I'll leave you alone.

Narrator 1: Bee continued his search, biting and tasting every creature he came to, including a horse, a pig, a rabbit, a cow, and a deer. But none of them tasted good.

Narrator 2: After a long while, Bee came to a man. He landed on the man's hand and bit him.

Man: Hey, little bee, why did you bite me?

Bee: Delbegen sent me to find the sweetest creature for him to eat, and I think I have just found him!

Man: You have? Who is it?

Bee: *You!* Nothing I've tasted is sweeter than you!

Narrator 1: Bee was happy that he had found the sweetest creature for Delbegen, and he began to sing a song.

Bee: (*singing*) Man is the sweetest. Man is the sweetest.

Man: Please, little bee, don't tell Delbegen that I am the sweetest. I don't want to be eaten by the giant.

Narrator 2: But the bee ignored the man and kept singing his song.

Bee: (*singing*) Man is the sweetest. Man is the sweetest.

Narrator 1: As the bee flew around, a brave man named Sartak-Pai heard the song.

Sartak-Pai: Why are you singing a song about "man is the sweetest?" What does that mean?

Bee: Delbegen, the giant with seven heads, asked me to find the sweetest creature on earth. I've tasted many, but man is the sweetest. Now I'll fly home to tell Delbegen.

Sartak-Pai: Why does Delbegen want to know?

Bee: So he can eat him, of course! From now on, Delbegen will only eat man because he is so sweet.

Sartak-Pai: Do you have to tell him?

Bee: Oh, yes! Now, if you'll excuse me, I must be on my way to Delbegen. (*singing*) Man is the sweetest. Man is the sweetest.

Narrator 2: But before the bee could get very far, Sartak-Pai grabbed him by his wings and tore out his tongue.

Sartak-Pai: Now, little bee, go to Delbegen, but you won't be able to sing your song.

Narrator 1: The bee flew away over lakes and hills, until at last he came to Delbegen.

Delbegen: I'm glad to see you, Bee. Now tell me, which creature is the sweetest?

Narrator 2: The bee wanted to sing, "Man is the sweetest," but when he opened his mouth, with no tongue, he couldn't sing anything.

Narrator 1: The only thing he could say was . . .

Bee: Bzzz. Bzzz. Bzzz.

Narrator 2: And to this day, the bumblebee can't say anything else.

How Spider Got His Narrow Waist

Summary

When Grandfather Spider hears there will be a feast in the jungle, he calls his grandchildren to help him find out more about it. Each of his four grandchildren tells him about a feast soon to come in their part of the jungle—east, west, north, and south. Not knowing the exact time of each feast, Grandfather devises a plan that will allow each grandchild to notify him. This tale, from Africa, has several renditions. RL3

Presentation Suggestions

Consider having the narrators split, with one on each side. Grandfather Spider should be in the center. When the bee and ant read, consider having them step forward, or enter from the side and leave after they have read. The drum could be off to one side. The four spider grandchildren could be slightly off center, close to Grandfather Spider.

Props

Perhaps the reader for drum could actually have a drum, and beat it in rhythm with his words. The bee could hold a jar of honey and the ant could hold a bag of rice.

Delivery

If possible, when Grandfather Spider asks about the feast, he could read quickly and sound excited. When the drum reads and sends his message, he should maintain a slow, steady, monotonous voice. When Grandfather Spider is squeezed by the threads, he should sound upset and in pain.

Related Books

Berman, Ruth. *Spinning Spiders.* Minneapolis, MN: Lerner Publications, 1998.
Carle, Eric. *The Very Busy Spider.* New York: Philomel, 1984.
Hovanec, Erin M. *Wonder What It's Like to Be a Spider.* New York: PowerKids Press, 2000.
MacDonald, Amy. *The Spider Who Created the Word.* New York: Orchard Books, 1996.
Platt, Richard. *Spider's Secrets.* New York: Dorling Kindersly, 2002.

Characters

Narrator 1

Narrator 2

Grandfather Spider (G. Spider)

Bee

Ant

Drum

Spider from the East

Spider from the West

Spider from the North

Spider from the South

How Spider Got His Narrow Waist

Narrator 1: One sunny spring day, Grandfather Spider walked through the jungle looking for something to eat. You see, Grandfather Spider was always hungry, and whenever he saw food, he ate it. That's why he had such a fat middle!

Narrator 2: As he walked, he saw many bees in the flowers collecting pollen to make honey.

G. Spider: Why do you want to make so much honey?

Bee: We're getting ready for the feast.

Narrator 1: When Grandfather Spider heard there was going to be a feast, he got excited. He loved feasts. It meant there would be a lot of food.

G. Spider: Feast? What feast? Who's having a feast? Where will it be? When will it be?

Narrator 2: The bees were too busy to answer Grandfather Spider, so he began to run through the jungle. He went to the anthill to ask the ants.

G. Spider: Ants run all over the jungle, and they always know what's going on. I'll ask them about the feast.

Narrator 1: As he neared the anthill, Grandfather Spider saw some ants running from the colony, while others were returning with a grain of rice, a green leaf, a mushroom, or a berry.

G. Spider: Why are you gathering so much food?

Ant: It's for the big feast.

G. Spider: Feast? What feast? Who's having a feast? Where will it be? When will it be?

Narrator 2: But the ants were too busy hurrying back and forth to answer.

G. Spider: I *must* find out about this feast. I'll send for my grandchildren to help me.

Narrator 1: Grandfather Spider ran to the tree where he lived. He scurried up the trunk and spun a heavy web between two branches.

Narrator 2: Then he wrapped soft leaves around a twig and beat it against the tight web.

Drum: Come home at once. Come home at once. Come home at once.

Narrator 1: He repeated the message over and over. It traveled fast and four of his grandchildren quickly arrived.

Narrator 2: One came from the east side of the jungle, and one from the west side. The other two came from the north and the south sides.

East Spider: I left home as soon as I heard your call.

West Spider: I came as soon as I got your message.

North Spider: Your message sounded urgent, Grandfather.

South Spider: Why did you call us?

G. Spider: I understand there will be a big feast, but I don't know who is having it, or when, or where, or why. Can any of you tell me?

East Spider: Recently I heard that Lion is getting married and is planning a wedding party in the east side in two or three days.

West Spider: From the west side of the jungle, Elephant is going to have a big birthday party sometime this week. But I don't know exactly when it will be.

North Spider: In the north end of the jungle, I heard that monkey is planning a feast for some of his friends. It should be soon.

South Spider: And from the south Zebra is going to celebrate the birth of her baby as soon as it is born.

G. Spider: Oh my! Four wonderful feasts in one week! That's exciting, and I'd like to go to all of them. I wonder which one I should go to first. Should I go east, or west, or north, or south? How will I know?

Narrator 2: Grandfather thought long and hard over what to do, and finally came up with a plan that would allow him to eat at all four feasts.

Narrator 1: He spun four long, strong, silken threads. He tied one end of each thread around his middle, and gave the other ends to his grandchildren.

G. Spider: Tie the end of the thread I gave you around your waist and return home. When you hear that the feast is beginning, pull hard on the thread. When I feel your pull, I'll know in which direction to travel.

Narrator 2: With a thread tied around their middle, the grandchildren went back to their parts of the jungle. Grandfather Spider was pleased with his plan. With luck, he'd be able to attend all four feasts.

Narrator 1: He waited for the first pull, and dreamed of all the food he'd soon be eating. Then, two days later, it came! A pull from the east.

G. Spider: Wonderful! Lion is married and ready to celebrate. I'll go at once.

Narrator 2: Just as Grandfather Spider started to head east, he felt a tug from the west.

G. Spider: Oh dear, it looks like Elephant's birthday party is about to begin. Now I have to make a choice.

Narrator 1: Before he could make a decision, Grandfather Spider felt a yank from the north.

G. Spider: This isn't fair! Monkey is having his feast for friends at the same time. Now what should I do?

Narrator 2: At that moment, he felt a hard yank from the south.

G. Spider: Looks like Zebra had her baby! Guess I'll head south.

Narrator 1: The grandchildren continued to pull, yank, and tug on their threads.

Narrator 2: Grandfather Spider was getting confused.

G. Spider: I'm going east. (*pause*) No, I'm going west. (*pause*) Nope, I guess I'm going north. (*pause*) Wrong again, I'll head south.

Narrator 1: Each time a thread was pulled, Grandfather Spider was squeezed, and it hurt!

G. Spider: Ouch! Stop! *Everyone, stop pulling. You're squeezing me in half.*

Narrator 2: But his grandchildren were too far away to hear his cries, and they continued to pull harder.

Narrator 1: The threads got tighter, Grandfather Spider's waist got smaller, and then—

Both Narrators: SNAP!

Narrator 2: All four threads snapped.

Narrator 1: Now Grandfather's big, fat waist was tiny.

Narrator 2: And to this day, all spiders have narrow waists.

How Butterflies Came to Be

Summary

This Native American tale (Papago tribe) describes how Elder Brother put together the colors from flowers and trees and other things from nature to create a new creature. RL4

Presentation Suggestions

The narrators could stand together off to one side. Elder Brother should be centrally located. The children should be grouped together, with the songbirds grouped together a short distance away.

Props

Elder Brother could wear a neutral color (brown or tan). The children and songbirds could be colorfully dressed. Perhaps a bag filled with paper butterflies could be near Elder Brother. He could hand the bag to one of the children, who could shake out the butterflies at the appropriate time.

Delivery

Elder Brother's voice should be smooth and warm. The children and birds should find a voice they like, making sure that there are variations in pitch, tone, and volume level.

Related Books

Cutts, David. *Look . . . a Butterfly.* Mahwah, NJ: Troll Books, 1982.
Delaney, A. *The Butterfly.* New York: Crown Publishing, 1977.
Gomi, Taro. *Hi, Butterfly!* New York: Morrow, 1985.
Hariton, Anca. *Butterfly Story.* New York: Dutton, 1995.
Ling, Mary. *Butterfly.* New York: Dorling Kindersley, 1992.

Characters

Narrator 1
Narrator 2
Elder Brother
Child 1

Child 2
Child 3
Child 4
Songbird 1
Songbird 2

How Butterflies Came to Be

Narrator 1: Long ago, Earth-Maker shaped the world. He made many beautiful animals, trees, and flowers.

Narrator 2: He also made Elder Brother.

Narrator 1: One day, Elder Brother went for a walk.

Narrator 2: It was just after the time of year when the rains came. Everything he saw was wonderful and beautiful.

Elder Brother: The flowers have so many lovely colors, and the trees are green and bright. The children, too, are beautiful as they play and sing.

Child 1: Hi, Elder Brother. Will you play with us?

Child 2: We can do anything you want.

Elder Brother: Thank you, children. I would like to play with you, but not now. I have things I must do.

Child 1: When you're finished, come back and we'll play.

Narrator 1: The children smiled at Elder Brother, and he smiled at them.

Elder Brother: What beautiful faces the children have. Their smiles light up their faces.

Narrator 1: Suddenly, Elder Brother stopped smiling, and he became sad.

Elder Brother: Someday, these beautiful young children will grow old and weak and die. And the beautiful red and yellow and white and blue flowers will fade. Soon, the leaves will fall from the trees. The days will grow short and the nights will be cold. But, I suppose that's the way it's meant to be. Even so, it's sad, so sad.

Narrator 2: Just then, a wind came along. It brushed past Elder Brother and made some of the yellow leaves fall from a tree.

Narrator 1: As the leaves fell, they looked like they were dancing in the sunlight.

Elder Brother: Seeing the leaves dance gives me an idea! I'll make something that will make the hearts of the children dance. It will also make my heart glad again.

Narrator 2: Elder Brother took a bag and put many bright-colored flowers and fallen leaves into it.

Narrator 1: Then he added yellow pollen, white cornmeal, and green pine needles to the bag.

Narrator 2: He caught some of the shining gold of the sunlight and put that into the bag.

Elder Brother: I have many beautiful things in this bag, but I need one thing more. I must add the songs of the birds.

Narrator 1: He took some of the songs from the birds and placed them into the bag.

Narrator 2: Then he went to the children.

Elder Brother: Come children, look what I have for you.

Narrator 1: The children gathered around him.

Child 1: What?

Child 2: Looks like a bag to me.

Child 3: What's in the bag, Elder Brother?

Narrator 2: He handed them his bag.

Elder Brother: Here, open this. You will find something special in the bag.

Narrator 1: The children opened Elder Brother's bag and out flew the first butterflies.

Narrator 2: Their wings were bright as sunlight and had all of the colors of the flowers and leaves. They also held the colors of cornmeal, pollen, and green pine needles.

Child 1: Oh, look! These creatures have so many pretty colors.

Child 2: I see red and gold and black and yellow . . .

Child 3: . . . and blue and green and white.

Child 4: They look like flowers dancing in the wind.

Narrator 1: The butterflies flew about the heads of the children and the children laughed.

Narrator 2: As those first butterflies flew, they sang beautiful songs, just like the birds.

Narrator 1: The children listened to the songs and danced to them.

Narrator 2: As the children listened to the singing butterflies, the songbirds came to Elder Brother.

Songbird 1: Elder Brother, why are those creatures singing our songs? They were given to us.

Songbird 2: We're happy to see the beautiful colors you have given these new creatures, but it is not right that you should also give them our songs.

Elder Brother: I never thought about that. You are right. The songs belong to you and not to the butterflies. I will take care of that right away.

Narrator 1: Elder Brother removed the songs from the butterflies, and to this day, butterflies fly and dance silently.

Narrator 2: When children see them dancing in the wind with their beautiful colors, their hearts are glad.

Both Narrators: And, that is how Elder Brother meant it to be.

Why Ants Are Found Everywhere

Summary

Ant arrives late at a celebration to honor Lion, king of the beasts. When he arrives he is ridiculed and sent home. Ant Queen, angered by the way Ant was treated, sends Worm to enter Lion's ear and make him miserable. Lion gets relief when Ant returns. In appreciation, Lion tells Ant that all ants can now live anywhere they wish. This story is from Burma. RL5

Presentation Suggestions

Because of the number of readers, it would be best to have both narrators together off to one side. Lion should be a short distance away, with the animals in a staggered formation in order of appearance. Consider having the ant enter from the side when the narrator introduces him. Ant can return to the side after reading. Ant Queen should stand and read her lines from the side. Consider having the messenger step forward from his position in the second row of the staggered line, and when he's finished, return to his position.

Props

Perhaps, if possible, each animal could be symbolically dressed, in appropriate colors with tails, ears, or spots. Lion could sit in an armed chair as his throne, and perhaps wear a king's crown.

Delivery

Animal voices should vary in pitch and volume, according to the size of the animal. Lion's voice should be loud, deep, and husky; voices for Ant and Ant Queen should be higher pitched; Snake should try to draw out the "s" sounds in his words to sound like hissing. Giraffe should use a stage whisper.

Related Books

Demuth, Patricia Brennan. *Those Amazing Ants.* New York: McMillan, 1994.
Korman, Justine. *A Bug's Life.* New York: Golden Books, 1998.
Moses, Amy. *If I Were an Ant.* San Francisco, CA: Children's Press, 1992.
Van Allsburg, Chris. *Two Bad Ants.* Boston: Houghton Mifflin, 1988.
Werber, Bernard. *Empire of the Ants.* New York: Bantam Books, 1998.
Wolkstein, Diane. *Step by Step.* New York: Morrow, 1994.

Characters

Narrator 1
Narrator 2
Lion
Tiger
Elephant
Snake
Lizard
Ant
Giraffe
Ant Queen
Worm
Messenger

Why Ants Are Found Everywhere

Narrator 1: In a time long ago, when animals could speak, Lion roared an order to all of the animals.

Lion: I am the king of beasts, and I want all animals to come and honor me. We'll have a celebration with plenty of food.

Narrator 2: All the animals heard Lion's order and immediately set out to see him. They arrived and lined up in front of Lion to honor him.

Tiger: Your highness, in your honor, I bow to you.

Elephant: I bow to you, oh mighty king, and thank you for inviting me to honor you.

Snake: It's a pleasure to be here and honor you, sire.

Lizard: Thank you for giving me the opportunity to honor you.

Narrator 1: The long line that formed in front of Lion gradually shortened as the animals moved forward.

Narrator 2: After the last animal had paid his respect to Lion, the king of beasts made an announcement.

Lion: I am delighted that you have all come to honor me. Always remember I am your king and will rule wisely. And now, let the celebration begin!

Narrator 1: The animals enjoyed the delicious food of different fruits, seeds, and roots, and ate heartily.

Narrator 2: Meanwhile, as the animals were eating, Ant was still working his way to see the king.

Narrator 1: It was a long, difficult journey for Ant. Every rock or vine he came to, he had to crawl up one side and down the other.

Ant: I never realized there were so many rocks and vines along the way. Each time it's like climbing up and down a mountain.

Narrator 2: And walking through the tall, thick grass was a real adventure.

Ant: This is like a jungle, or a maze. I hope I'm going in the right direction.

Narrator 1: Each small puddle he came to was like swimming across a huge lake.

Narrator 2: But Ant continued to walk, climb, and swim, hoping that he would get to Lion in time to honor him.

Narrator 1: Meanwhile, back at the celebration, all of the animals had eaten enough food, and their bellies were full. Now they began to sing and dance. Lion sat on his throne, looking over the happy throng of his subjects.

Lion: This is good! The animals have honored me, and now they are enjoying themselves. They will remember this celebration for a long time and continue to love and honor me.

Narrator 2: Giraffe, who was having a great time dancing with Elephant, noticed a small black object in the distance. It was moving toward them. He whispered to Elephant.

Giraffe: Look out there. I think Ant has finally arrived.

Elephant: You're right. Hey, everyone, look who's coming! It's Ant!

Narrator 1: All of the animals stopped dancing and looked at Ant. They made fun of him as he drew closer.

Tiger: Slowpoke! Slowpoke!

Snake: Shame on you, arriving late to honor the king!

Lizard: When you go somewhere, you'll have to learn to leave home earlier. Give yourself plenty of time for your journey.

Narrator 2: Lion laughed loudly and roared.

Lion: It's about time you got here, you foolish little thing. You're not fit to stand before me. Go back home.

Narrator 1: Ant crawled away in shame and went home. He told the Queen of the Ants how badly Lion had treated him.

Narrator 2: The Ant Queen was *very* angry, and went to her friend, Worm.

Queen: I want you to go to Lion and crawl in his ear. Torture him. Stay there until I send you word to leave.

Worm: I'll go right away, dear friend. And I'll make that Lion wish he had never met Ant.

Narrator 1: When Worm reached Lion, he crept into the king's ear and wiggled and jiggled until he was deep inside.

Narrator 2: Lion was uncomfortable. He shook his head back and forth trying to get the worm out. He roared to the other animals.

Lion: Don't just stand there, do something!

Narrator 1: The animals didn't know what to do, and none of them was small enough to climb in Lion's ear.

Lion: This is making me crazy! If you can't help me, get someone who can!

Elephant: Who should we get?

Lion: There is only one animal I know that is small enough to go into my ear. Send a messenger to Ant.

Narrator 2: The messenger went to the Ant Queen.

Messenger: Please send someone to crawl into Lion's ear and get Worm out. Lion is miserable.

Queen: Very well. I suppose Lion has been punished enough, so I will send Ant to help him.

Narrator 1: Ant returned with the messenger, and when he finally arrived, he found Lion rolling on the ground in pain.

Lion: Hurry up! Crawl in my ear and get the worm out. It hurts badly!

Narrator 2: Ant crawled into Lion's ear and called out.

Ant: Worm, you can come out now. And thank you for helping me.

Narrator 1: Worm wiggled out and now Lion was free from pain.

Lion: Thank you, Ant. For doing me such a great service, I have decided that from now on you and your people may live anywhere you'd like.

Narrator 2: When Ant went home, he told Ant Queen what Lion had said. Soon after, many of the ants moved to other locations.

Narrator 1: Today, some animals live only in special places, like the jungle, or the desert, or in the rain forest.

Narrator 2: But ants live *everywhere*. And now you know why.

How Bean Got Its Stripe

Summary

A piece of straw, a lump of coal, and a bean escape from a fire and decide to travel together. When they stop by a brook, the straw's plan for crossing the water doesn't work out. The bean laughs so hard when it sees the coal and straw fall into the water that it splits its sides, but is sewn up by a traveling tailor. This is a tale from Germany. RL2

Presentation Suggestions

The narrators could be split, and the three main characters could stand in the center. Consider having the tailor stand at the side and step forward to read his lines.

Props

Straw could wear yellow, coal could wear black, and bean could wear brown. The tailor could hold up a needle and spool of black thread when the narrator talks about them.

Delivery

Through pitch, intonation, pacing, and volume, vary the voices of the straw, coal, and bean, giving each a distinctive characterization.

Related Books

Green, Aliza. *The Bean Bible*. Philadelphia, PA: Running Press, 2000.
Lewis, Beverly. *Big Bad Beans*. Minneapolis, MN: Bethany House, 2000.
Miller, Susanna. *Beans and Peas*. Minneapolis, MN: Carolrhoda Books, 1990.
Osborne, Mary Pope. *Kate and the Beanstalk*. New York: Atheneum, 2000.
Rockwell, Anne. *One Bean*. New York: Walker & Co, 1998.

Characters

Narrator 1
Narrator 2
Straw

Coal

Bean

Tailor

How Bean Got Its Stripe

Narrator 1: There was once a time when *everything* could talk, not just people or animals.

Narrator 2: In this story, a long straw, a glowing coal, and a bean talk. Listen to what they have to say as they talk around a fire in an old woman's home.

Straw: Boy, that was a close call! I was able to slip through the old lady's fingers before she could throw me into the fire. Otherwise, I would have been burned to a crisp and be nothing but smoke in the chimney.

Coal: I was already in the fire but jumped out. If I had stayed there, I'd be history! As it is, I'm still glowing from the fire.

Narrator 1: Just then, another voice spoke. It was Bean, who had fallen out of a pot of boiling water hanging over the fire.

Bean: Whew! That was too close for comfort! I was really in hot water and didn't like it one bit! Why, if I hadn't jumped out, I'd be cooked and the old woman would have eaten me.

Coal: We're all lucky to have escaped from the fire. Now what shall we do?

Bean: This is certainly no place for any of us, so we must get away. Let's travel!

Straw: I like that idea, Bean. I've never been anywhere.

Coal: Now you're cooking! Whoops—I didn't mean that the way it sounded.

Bean: That's okay, I know what you mean. Let's get going.

Narrator 2: The three of them ran out the open door, down the road, and into the nearby woods.

Narrator 1: Soon they came to a small running brook and stopped, not knowing what to do next.

Straw: No water for me, thank you. That current is too swift and would sweep me away to who-knows-where.

Coal: If I go into the water, I know I'd sink to the bottom. That would be the end of me.

Bean: I don't know how to swim and I don't want to find out what would happen if I went into the water.

Straw: I've got an idea! I'll lay myself over the brook like a bridge. Then you both can go across.

Narrator 2: Straw stretched itself from bank to bank and told Coal and Bean to cross over.

Coal: I'll go first.

Narrator 1: Coal walked to the middle of the brook and heard the running water underneath.

Coal: Oh dear. What if I fall in? I know I'll drown, I just know it!

Narrator 2: So Coal stopped and just stood there, not able to move another step. The heat from Coal made Straw catch fire. Straw burned and broke in two, and they both fell into the water.

Narrator 1: Bean watched as Straw burned up and Coal sank to the bottom of the brook with a hiss.

Bean: This is a terrible thing to happen! But you both look funny! Forgive me for laughing, but I can't help myself—I have to! (*laugh long and hard*).

Narrator 2: Bean laughed so hard it burst! That would have been the end of it, except just then, a tailor came along.

Tailor: You poor little bean, you've split your sides. It's a good thing for you that I'm here. I'll fix you up as good as new.

Narrator 1: The tailor took out a needle and black thread and sewed up the bean's split sides.

Narrator 2: And that is why, to this day, some beans have black seams.

Why Some Trees Are Always Green

Summary

The trees enter a contest to see who can stay awake for seven nights. The winners remain green all year long. This tale is from the Cherokee tribe. RL2

Presentation Suggestions

Both narrators could stand together off to one side of the stage. Trees should be centrally located, in a staggered row. Consider having Maker stand in the center of the stage in the beginning, then move to the side after reading the first lines. Toward the end, Maker could return to the center for the final reading.

Props

If desired, trees of oak tag or cardboard could be placed around the area. Trees 1, 2, and 3 could dress in green, while the other trees could wear brown or tan. Maker should wear white or neutral colors.

Delivery

Each tree should try to find a different-sounding voice, varying in pitch, volume, or pacing. Maker should have a deep, smooth voice.

Related Books

Kirkpatrick, Rena K. *Trees.* Milwaukee, WI: Raintree Children's Books, 1985.
Lauter, Patricia. *Being a Friend to Trees.* New York: HarperCollins, 1994.
Stone, Marti. *The Singing Fir Tree.* New York: Putnam, 1992.

Characters

Narrator 1
Narrator 2
Maker
Tree 1
Tree 2

Tree 3

Tree 4

Tree 5

Tree 6

Why Some Trees Are Always Green

Narrator 1: When plants and trees were first made, the Maker gave each species a special gift.

Narrator 2: Then he set up a contest to find out which gift would be most useful.

Maker: I want all of you to stay awake and keep watch over the earth for seven nights. Do you think you can do that?

Tree 1: Wow! This is great! Just think, we're going to stay up *all night* for seven nights.

Tree 2: That won't be hard to do!

Tree 3: I'm sure *I* can do it.

Narrator 1: The first night, all of the trees were so excited. None of them wanted to sleep, so they all stayed awake.

Narrator 2: Then came the second night.

Tree 4: I'm so tired.

Tree 5: I can hardly stay awake.

Tree 6: I'd love to go to sleep, but I know I shouldn't.

Narrator 1: Many of the trees wanted to sleep but didn't. But just before dawn of the third day, a few of them fell asleep.

Narrator 2: On the third night, it was harder for the trees to stay awake. They whispered to each other, trying to stay awake.

Tree 1: Do you think you'll fall asleep tonight?

Tree 2: I hope not.

Tree 3: If we keep talking, maybe we'll stay awake.

Narrator 1: The trees whispered in the wind, but it was too much work for some of them, and they dropped off to sleep.

Narrator 2: Only a few trees were still awake when the fourth night came.

Tree 4: I don't think I'm going to make it tonight. I can hardly stay awake.

Tree 5: Me too. Goodnight!

Tree 6: Staying awake for so many nights is hard to do.

Narrator 1: And one by one the trees fell asleep. In fact, almost all of them slept.

Narrator 2: Each night, more trees dropped off to sleep, until by the seventh night, the only trees that were still awake were the cedar, the pine, the spruce, the fir, the holly, and the laurel.

Maker: How strong you all are! Not one of you went to sleep for seven nights. That's wonderful, and I'm proud of all of you. I now give you the special gift of remaining green forever.

Narrator 1: The trees and plants were pleased with their gift.

Tree 1: We did it!

Tree 2: I knew we could!

Tree 3: Hooray for us!

Maker: All of you will always guard the forest. Your leaves will hold great medicine, and in the dead of winter, life will be protected in your branches.

Narrator 1: Ever since then, when the other trees and plants lose their leaves and sleep all winter, the evergreens stay awake.

Narrator 2: But that's not the end of the story. The panther and owl also stayed awake, so Maker gave them the power to see in the dark. Now they prey on animals that sleep.

Why the Oak Tree Keeps Its Leaves

Summary

When a buck that Swift Running Water shot dies on the land of the Old Man, the Indian must exchange his life for that of the deer. He makes an agreement with the Old Man to return to him when all of the trees are bare. His wife, Little Bird, pleads with trees in the forest to hold their leaves during the winter, but only the oak tree is willing to try. It is successful, and the life of the young Indian is spared. This is an original tale by the author of this book. RL4

Presentation Suggestions

The narrators could be split, one on each side of the stage. The main characters could stand in the center, in this suggested order: Old Man, Swift Running Water, Little Bird. The trees could be off to one side. When each tree speaks, the reader could step forward, then back in place when finished.

Props

If possible, have a couple of trees (oak tag or cardboard) off to one side. Swift Running Water could wear a headband with a feather and have a bow and arrow strapped to him. The Old Man could wear tan clothing, moccasins, and a plain headband. Little Bird could wear a beaded necklace. The maple tree and oak tree could have colorful leaves pinned onto their shirts.

Delivery

The Old Man's voice should be deep with a deliberate reading. The maple tree's voice could be soft and shaky, while the oak tree's voice could be strong and confident.

Related Books

Coats, Laura Jane. *The Oak Tree*. New York: Macmillan, 1987.
Fleisher, Paul. *The Oak Tree*. New York: Marshall Cavendish, 1998.
Kottke, Jan. *From Acorns to Oak Tree*. Danbury, CT: Children's Press, 2000.
Royston, Angela. *Life Cycle of an Oak Tree*. Chicago: Heinemann Library, 2000.

Characters

Narrator 1
Narrator 2
Swift Running Water
Old Man
Little Bird
Maple Tree
Oak Tree

Why the Oak Tree Keeps Its Leaves

Narrator 1: In a time long ago, trees developed their leaves in the spring, were full in the summer, and dropped their leaves in the fall. This was the cycle of trees.

Narrator 2: But that cycle changed for one tree, as you are about to hear.

Narrator 1: Early one fall, Swift Running Water was hunting for food for his wife, Little Bird, and infant son. He had already killed several small animals for winter food, but needed a larger one, like a deer.

Narrator 2: Swift Running Water walked quietly and carefully through the woods.

Swift: I must be careful not to step on any fallen leaves or twigs. They would crunch under my feet and the forest animals would know I'm here.

Narrator 1: Finally, the young Indian came to a clearing. He dropped to one knee and scanned the area. He was delighted with what he saw standing close to the forest on the other side of the clearing.

Swift: There is one of the largest and most beautiful deer I've ever seen! That buck would provide many fine meals for my family throughout the winter, and Little Bird could make clothing from its hide for us.

Narrator 2: Now on hands and knees, his bow and arrow strapped to his back, Swift Running Water crawled across the meadow.

Narrator 1: Occasionally he raised his head to make sure the buck was still there, then continued crawling until he was a few yards from the deer.

Narrator 2: The Indian lifted himself to one knee, took an arrow from its quiver, and inserted it into the bow. He drew back the string of the bow and aimed.

Narrators: (*together*) *Zing!*

Swift: Good! My arrow found its mark and the deer has fallen. My wife will be pleased when she sees me bring this buck home.

Narrator 1: Just then, the deer managed to push itself from the ground. It stood on wobbly legs for a minute, then turned and ran into the woods behind him.

Swift: No! This can't be. I saw the deer fall. I'm sure it was dead. But, although it managed to get to its feet, I know it is wounded. It won't be able to go very far or fast. I must run after it.

Narrator 2: Swift Running Water ran across the clearing and into the forest. He followed the sounds of the buck as it crashed through the woods.

Narrator 1: He soon caught up with the deer and watched as it jumped over a narrow stream of water, then fell on the other side.

Narrator 2: Within minutes, Swift Running Water was next to the buck. It did not move. The young Indian picked up the hind legs of the deer, one in each hand. With the deer behind him, Swift Running Water began to drag the buck.

Swift: I must get to the other side of this stream where I will be safe. On this side, the land belongs to the Old Man, and his law is well known—if an animal is killed on the Old Man's land, the one who killed it must give *his* life in return.

Narrator 1: With his head bent down, Swift Running Water pulled the heavy buck toward the stream.

Narrator 2: But before he reached the water, he saw a pair of moccasins in front of him. Slowly, he looked up, until his eyes met the eyes of the Old Man.

Old Man: I see you have a deer that died on my land.

Swift: Yes, I do. But I shot it on the other side of your land. It ran here, where it died.

Old Man: I am not concerned with where you shot it. I am concerned with where it *died*. And, it died on my land. Do you know the punishment for causing the death of any animal on my land?

Swift: Your law is well known. I am prepared to give you my life in exchange for that of the deer. But since it is dead, may I first bring it to my family so they will have meat for the cold winter months that lie ahead?

Old Man: I will consent to that. When will you return to me?

Swift: When all of the trees have lost their leaves and they are bare.

Narrator 1: The Old Man agreed, and Swift Running Water continued home with the buck.

Narrator 2: When he was near his village, Little Bird ran to greet him.

Little Bird: My husband, I see you have brought us meat—a fine, big buck.

Narrator 1: Then noticing the sad look on her husband's face, she asked what was wrong.

Narrator 2: Swift Running Water told her how the buck had died on the Old Man's land, and of the agreement he had made with the Old Man.

Little Bird: We must think of something so you will not have to give your life to the Old Man.

Narrator 1: That night, as Little Bird lie next to her husband, she came up with a plan. When the sun shed the first light of day, the young Indian woman rose and quietly left her sleeping husband.

Narrator 2: She went into the forest and approached a maple tree, whose branches were filled with colorful leaves.

Little Bird: Beautiful maple tree, I need your help. My husband killed a deer that died on the Old Man's land. Now he must return to the Old Man when the trees have lost their leaves. Do you think you could hold on to your leaves this winter?

Maple Tree: I wish I could, but the winter wind is too strong. I would not be able to keep my leaves no matter how hard I try. I'm sorry.

Narrator 1: Little Bird next went to an elm tree, which also could not help her.

Narrator 2: She went deeper into the forest, going from tree to tree. Each time she told her story and each time she got the same answer: None of the trees felt that they could hold their leaves against the strong winter wind.

Narrator 1: Now there was only the oak tree left. Tearfully, she approached the massive tree and told her story for the last time.

Oak Tree: I don't know if I'll be able to hold my leaves or not, but I'll try.

Narrator 2: With hope in her heart, Little Bird returned to her husband and told him of her efforts and the result.

Narrator 1: As winter approached, one by one the trees lost their leaves. Swift Running Water and his wife kept watch over the oak tree, which still held most of its leaves.

Narrator 2: Then one day, the Old Man came to visit Swift Running Water.

Old Man: The trees are bare, and you did not come to me as you promised. So I have come for you.

Swift: My promise was to come to you when *all* of the trees are bare. Look at the oak tree— it still has its leaves.

Old Man: Well, when the oak tree has lost its leaves, then you must come. I'll wait for you.

Narrator 1: Winter passed and again the Old Man returned to Swift Running Water.

Old Man: Why didn't you come to me when the oak tree no longer had its leaves? You have broken your promise.

Swift: No I haven't. If you look at the trees, you'll see they have new leaves on them. There was never a time when *all* of the trees were bare.

Old Man: You are very clever and fortunate. I release you from your promise, but now I seek a new one from you. *Never step on my land again!*

Swift: I promise, and I thank you for your fairness.

Narrator 2: The Old Man returned to his home and never saw Swift Running Water again.

Narrator 1: Swift Running Water and Little Bird spent many happy hours and years with their son under the branches of the strong oak tree.

Narrator 2: They thought of the great tree as a member of their family—one who fought the winter wind, held on to its leaves, and saved the life of Swift Running Water.

Narrator 1: Since that time, when trees drop their leaves in winter, the oak tree continues to hold its leaves.

Narrator 2: And now you know why.

Why Frog Cries at Night

Summary

A monkey and a frog decide to live together and avoid being lonely. But it doesn't work out the way they had hoped. RL1

Presentation Suggestions

The narrators could be close together off to one side. Monkey should be in the center of the stage area. The snake, deer, and frog could be on the opposite side. Frog could walk to the monkey and read his part from that position.

Props

Monkey could wear brown, the frog could wear green, the deer could wear tan, and the snake could wear brown or green. If possible, the deer could wear a headband of antlers and the monkey could wear a long tail.

Delivery

Voices should differ in pitch and attempt to mimic the animals they represent. The frog should sound a bit croaky or raspy, and the snake should have a hissing sound when he speaks. The monkey could speak rapidly, as though he were chattering.

Related Books

Arnosky, Jim. *All About Frogs.* 2002. New York: Scholastic, 2002.
Goss, Linda. *The Frog Who Wanted to Be a Singer.* New York: Orchard Books, 1995.
Royston, Angela. *See How They Grow—The Frog.* New York: Dorling Kindersly, 2001.
Tagholm, Sally. *Animal Lives—The Frog.* New York: Kingfisher, 2000.

Characters

Narrator 1
Narrator 2
Monkey

Snake
Deer
Frog

Why Frog Cries at Night

Narrator 1: Monkey lived alone in a tree.

Narrator 2: He didn't like living by himself.

Monkey: I'm going to take a walk. Maybe I'll find someone to live with.

Narrator 1: Monkey walked into the woods and came to a snake.

Monkey: Hello, Snake. I live alone and don't like it. Would you live with me?

Snake: No thank you. I have a very nice home in a hole in the ground.

Narrator 2: Monkey walked on until he met a deer.

Monkey: I'm looking for someone to live with me. Would you like to live with me, Deer?

Deer: I can't climb trees, Monkey. Besides, I have a family to take care of.

Narrator 1: Monkey was sad. He couldn't find anyone to live with him.

Monkey: I've got to find someone to live with me. I'll keep walking. There are other animals in the woods. I'm sure one of them would want to live with me.

Narrator 2: Soon, Monkey saw Frog. Frog was lonely, too.

Frog: Hello, Monkey. I'm glad to see you. You see I live alone. Would you like to live with me?

Monkey: Really? This is my lucky day. I'm looking for someone to live with me, too.

Frog: Then let's do it! Let's live together. It's not good to live alone.

Narrator 1: So, Monkey and Frog lived together for many weeks.

Narrator 2: All went well, until one night when it started to rain.

Monkey: It's raining very hard. I don't like so much rain.

Frog: The rain is cold. I don't like cold rain.

Narrator 1: It rained all night. Both of them were cold and unhappy. Frog cried all night. Monkey couldn't sleep.

Narrator 2: In the morning, the rain stopped. The sun came out.

Monkey: This is *much* better.

Frog: I don't ever want to be cold again. I think we should work together to make a warm coat. Then, if it gets cold at night, we'll be warm.

Monkey: That's a good idea, Frog.

Frog: First, I want to sit in the sun. I need to get warm and sleep a little bit.

Narrator 1: Frog sat in the sun all day, getting warm and sleeping.

Narrator 2: That night, it rained again.

Frog: Brrr, I'm so cold.

Monkey: We should have made a warm coat like you said. But instead of working, you wanted to sit in the sun all day.

Frog: How was I to know it would rain again tonight?

Monkey: Tomorrow we *must* make a warm coat.

Narrator 1: The next day, the rain stopped and the sun came out.

Narrator 2: Again, Frog sat in the sun all day. He didn't want to make a warm coat.

Narrator 1: This went on for many days.

Monkey: That's it, Frog. I can't live with you anymore.

Frog: Why? What did I do?

Monkey: You cry all night because you're cold and I can't sleep. All day you sit in the sun and won't work on a warm coat.

Frog: I guess we can't live together after all.

Monkey: That's right. It's better for me to live alone in the top of a tree than to listen to you cry all night.

Narrator 2: To this day, Frog sits in the sun in the daytime, where he sleeps and is warm. But at night, when it rains, he gets cold and cries.

Why Frog and Snake Never Play Together

Summary

A frog and a snake meet and play together, not realizing they should be enemies. When their mothers inform them, they are unable to remain friends. This is a Nigerian tale. RL2

Presentation Suggestions

Narrators could read from opposite sides of the stage. Frog and Snake should stand in the center. Frog's mother should stand slightly behind and off to one side of Frog; Snake's mother should stand slightly behind and off to one side of Snake.

Props

Some plants could surround the stage area, to give the feel of woods. The frogs could wear green, while the snakes could wear colorful clothing.

Delivery

Frog and his mother could talk with a throaty quality, almost like croaking. Snake and his mother could draw out their words, especially those that have an "s" in them. If desired, the snakes could inject a *hisss* every now and again, where appropriate.

Related Books

Bryan, Ashley. *Beat the Story-Drum, Pum Pum.* New York: Macmillan, 1980.
Faulkner, Keith. *The Snake's Mistake.* New York: Macmillan, 1988.
Goss, Linda. *The Frog Who Wanted to Be a Singer.* New York: Orchard Books, 1995.
Hawes, Judy. *Why Frogs Are Wet.* New York: HarperCollins, 2000.
Parsons, Alexandra. *Amazing Snakes.* New York: Alfred A. Knopf, 1990.

Characters

Narrator 1
Narrator 2
Frog

Snake
Mother Frog
Mother Snake

Why Frog and Snake Never Play Together

Narrator 1: One sunny day, Frog went for a walk in the woods. On the path ahead of him, he saw something new—something he had never seen before.

Narrator 2: It was long and thin, and it had a shiny coat with many colors.

Frog: Hello. Who are you?

Snake: I am Snake. Who are you?

Frog: I am Frog. Would you like to play with me?

Narrator 1: Frog and Snake played together and had fun.

Snake: I like the way you hop, Frog. Will you show me how to do it?

Frog: Sure, if you'll show me how to crawl on my belly like you do.

Narrator 2: So, Frog taught Snake how to hop, and Snake taught Frog how to crawl. They hopped and crawled all morning until they both felt hungry.

Frog: I have to go home now to eat lunch, but I'd like to play with you again.

Snake: I'd like to play with you, too. Let's meet tomorrow morning, right here.

Narrator 1: They agreed and each headed home. When Frog reached his home, he eagerly showed his mother how he could crawl on his belly.

Mother Frog: Where did you learn to do that?

Frog: I met Snake this morning and he taught me how to do it. Isn't it cool?

Mother Frog: No! Snake is a bad family. They have poison in their teeth. Don't ever play with him again! And I don't want to see you crawl on your belly again, either.

Narrator 2: Meanwhile, at his home, Snake showed his mother how he could hop.

Mother Snake: Where did you learn to hop like that?

Snake: I played with Frog this morning, and he showed me how to do it. Look how high I can hop! But Frog can hop higher.

Mother Snake: Frog? You played with Frog? Don't you know that Snakes don't play with Frogs? Snakes eat Frogs. Next time you're with Frog, grab him and eat him. And don't ever hop again!

Narrator 1: The next morning Frog and Snake kept their promise to each other and met in the woods.

Narrator 2: But they each thought about what their mothers had said, and did not get close to each other.

Frog: Snake, I'm sorry to tell you this, but I can't play with you any more.

Snake: And I can't play with you, either. We had fun yesterday, didn't we?

Frog: Yeah. It's too bad we can't have fun today, too. Now we have to say good-bye. And I guess we won't ever see each other again.

Narrator 1: Sadly, they left each other. After that, they often sat alone in the sun thinking about their one day of friendship and how much fun they had.

Narrator 2: And they wonder what would have happened if they had never told their mothers about each other. Why, they might still be playing together!

Narrator 1: But of course, they don't.

Narrator 2: And now you know why Frog and Snake never play together.

Why Turtle's Shell Is Cracked

Summary

Based on a tale from India, this story relates how a talkative turtle, traveling south with two robins transporting him on a stick, cannot refrain from expressing his pleasure while flying over mountains. As soon as he opens his mouth, he begins to fall, finally landing in a pond where he sleeps all winter. When he awakes in the spring, the two robins appear again and notice the turtle's cracked shell. RL2

Presentation Suggestions

The two narrators could stand together on one side. Turtle should stand in the center, with the two robins standing a short distance away. The robins could move closer to the turtle when talking with him, move away when the turtle falls, and then move back to the turtle at the pond.

Props

A small tub or pail of water could be placed near the narrators. When they say "Splash!" they could hit the water with one hand.

Delivery

Turtle should speak slowly and deliberately, with a low, dragging voice. The two robins should speak in quicker, higher pitched voices.

Related Books

Domanska, Janina. *Look, There Is a Turtle Flying.* New York: Macmillan, 1968.
Harrison, David Lee. *Little Turtle's Big Adventure.* New York: Random House, 1985.
Ross, Gayle. *How Turtle's Back Was Cracked.* New York: Dial Books, 1995.

Characters

Narrator 1
Narrator 2

Turtle
Robin 1
Robin 2

Why Turtle's Shell Is Cracked

Narrator 1: There was once a turtle who loved to talk. He talked all the time—to *everything*.

Narrator 2: One chilly, fall day, two robins landed in front of the turtle.

Turtle: Hello, birds. Where are you going?

Robin 1: We're flying south.

Turtle: What's south?

Robin 2: It's not a "what"—it's a place.

Robin 1: A place where it's always warm.

Robin 2: Winter is coming, Turtle. Soon it will snow and be cold.

Robin 1: We don't like it when it's cold. That's why we're going south.

Turtle: That sounds nice. I wish I could go south and be warm too.

Robin 2: I have an idea! Why don't you go south with us?

Turtle: But I can't fly.

Robin 1: That's okay. We'll take you.

Narrator 2: The robins told Turtle to find a thick stick and bring it to them. Turtle walked around until he found a strong stick. He brought it back to the robins.

Turtle: How's this?

Robin 2: Perfect. Now put your mouth in the middle of the stick and hold on tight. Don't open your mouth for *anything*.

Narrator 1: Turtle did as he was told. He clamped his strong mouth around the middle of the stick. One of the robins held onto one end of the stick, and the other robin held onto the other end. Then up they flew, lifting the turtle into the air.

Narrator 2: Turtle looked down. For the first time in his life, he saw the tops of flowers and trees. This was wonderful!

Narrator 1: He wanted the robins to know how happy he was, so he flapped his feet hard and fast.

Narrator 2: But the birds didn't notice. They flew higher. Now the turtle saw the tops of houses. He had never seen the tops of houses before. He was excited. He moved his head quickly back and forth to let the birds know how much he liked flying high in the air.

Narrator 1: They still didn't notice. The birds flew higher. Now he saw lakes below. They looked like puddles. And he saw the tops of mountains. He had *never* seen mountains before!

Narrator 2: He opened his mouth to say, "This is fantastic," but as soon as he opened his mouth, Turtle let go of the stick. He began to fall.

Narrator 1: Turtle rolled over and over. He was scared. Turtle pulled his legs and head into his shell.

Narrator 2: As he fell, he dove down faster and faster, until he fell into a pond.

Narrators: (*together*) SPLASH!

Narrator 1: Turtle sank to the bottom of the pond where he slept all winter.

Narrator 2: In the spring, Turtle woke up and swam to the top of the pond. Then he swam to the side of the pond and climbed out onto the grass.

Narrator 1: Just then, the two robins came and landed in front of the turtle.

Robin 1: Hey, Turtle! We sure are glad to see you.

Robin 2: We're really sorry about your fall.

Narrator 2: One of the robins looked at Turtle's back.

Robin 1: What happened to your back?

Narrator 1: Turtle looked over his shoulder. His hard shell had many cracks all over it. And between the cracks, there was white scar tissue.

Turtle: Gosh, I must have cracked my shell when I fell.

Narrator 2: To this day, all turtles have cracked shells. And now you know why.

How the Turtle Got His Shell

Summary

There are many different stories that tell how the turtle got its shell, and most of them stem from the Native American Indians. In this rendition, the naked turtle is the only animal that successfully takes away the leopard's drum for Ruler of the Sky. As a reward, Ruler gives Turtle a hard shell for protection. RL3

Presentation Suggestions

The narrators could stand beside each other toward the front at one side of the stage area. Ruler of the Sky should be slightly off-center and the other animals should be slightly off-center opposite him. As each animal speaks, the reader could step forward, and when finished reading, step back into place. Leopard could be at the front, on the opposite side from the narrators to give some distance between him and the other animals. When Turtle returns with the drum, he could walk and stand close to Ruler of the Sky, so Ruler could place the shell on the turtle's back at the appropriate time.

Props

Someone could beat a drum (off stage)—a few steady beats—in the beginning to set the mood of the story. It could also be used at the end of the story. If possible, a cardboard shell could be made and placed over the turtle when Ruler grants his wish.

Delivery

Each animal should have a different voice quality, such as pitch, tone, pacing, or volume level. Turtle's voice should be higher pitched, and the leopard's voice should have a hoarse, growling quality. Ruler could have a regal quality, and sound strong and sure of himself.

Related Books

Arnosky, Jim. *All About Turtles*. New York: Scholastic, 2002.
Chottin, Ariane. *A Home for Little Turtle*. Pleasantville, NY: Reader's Digest, 1992.
McGuire-Turcotte, Casey A. *How Honu the Turtle Got His Shell*. New York: Raintree, 1991.
Murdocca, Sal. *Turtle's Shell*. New York: Mondo, 1999.
Yeoman, John, and Quentin Blake. *The Singing Tortoise and Other Animal Folktales*. New York: Tambourine Books, 1993.

Characters

Narrator 1
Narrator 2
Leopard
Ruler of the Sky
Elephant
Crocodile
Tiger
Turtle

How the Turtle Got His Shell

Narrator 1: A long time ago, when animals could talk, Leopard had a drum.

Narrator 2: It was a big, beautiful drum. And it was LOUD! Leopard was very proud of his drum.

Leopard: No one has a drum as grand or loud as mine.

Narrator 1: Leopard played his drum every day. All the animals heard it. And Ruler of the Sky heard it, too.

Narrator 2: Ruler of the Sky liked the drum very much. In fact, he liked it so much that he wished he could have Leopard's drum. One day, Ruler of the Sky called all the animals of the jungle to come to him.

Ruler: You hear Leopard play his drum, don't you? Have you ever heard anything so grand? It is certainly the loudest drum I have ever heard, and I want it. I *must* have Leopard's drum! Who will get it for me?

Narrator 1: The animals looked at each other to see who would make an offer. Then, Elephant stepped forward.

Elephant: As you can see, I am big. Leopard will be scared when he sees me. I'll get the drum for you, Ruler of the Sky.

Narrator 2: Elephant went to Leopard's home. When he got there, Leopard showed his long claws and sharp teeth and gave a long, deep growl.

Leopard: What do you want, Elephant?

Narrator 1: Elephant was scared. His voice shook when he answered.

Elephant: Nothing. I was just taking a walk. But now, I must go home.

Narrator 2: Elephant turned around and ran back to Ruler of the Sky.

Elephant: I'm sorry. I couldn't get Leopard's drum for you.

Narrator 1: Then Crocodile stepped forward.

Crocodile: I'll go, Ruler. Elephant couldn't get the drum, but when Leopard sees so many teeth in my mouth, he'll be scared. I'm sure he will give me his drum just to get rid of me.

Narrator 2: When Leopard saw Crocodile coming, he showed his long claws and sharp teeth and gave a long, deep growl.

Narrator 1: Crocodile didn't wait to hear what Leopard had to say. He quickly turned around and ran back home.

Crocodile: Sorry, Ruler. Something unexpected came up, and I didn't get the drum.

Narrator 2: Next, Tiger stepped forward.

Tiger: Have no fear, Ruler of the Sky. I know that Leopard will be so scared of me when he sees me coming that he'll let me have his drum.

Narrator 1: So, Tiger went to visit Leopard.

Narrator 2: But when Tiger saw Leopard's long claws and sharp teeth and heard the low growl, he was scared and ran back to Ruler of the Sky.

Tiger: I'm sorry, but I wasn't able to get Leopard's drum for you.

Narrator 1: One by one, the animals of the jungle went to Leopard, but none of them could get the drum.

Narrator 2: Ruler of the Sky was very disappointed.

Ruler: I *must* have Leopard's drum. Can't one of you get it for me?

Narrator 1: Then, Ruler heard a little voice. He looked around to see where the voice came from, and saw that it was Turtle who had spoken.

Turtle: I'll get the drum for you. You can count on me.

Narrator 2: Turtle was small and bare, for he had no covering on his body at all. When the animals looked at him, they all laughed.

All Animals: (*laugh long and hard*) Ha, ha, ha.

Elephant: Look at you! You're little and weak.

Tiger: If I couldn't get Leopard's drum, how do you think you can?

Turtle: I have a plan. I *know* I can get the drum.

Ruler: Very well, Turtle. None of the others were able to get the drum, but perhaps you can. At least you can try.

Narrator 1: Turtle went to see Leopard. When he got close to Leopard's home, he called out in his loudest voice.

Turtle: Hey, Leopard. Did you hear the latest news?

Leopard: What news is that?

Turtle: Ruler of the Sky now has a drum. It's much nicer and louder than yours.

Narrator 2: Leopard was so surprised at the news that he forgot to show his long claws and sharp teeth and growl.

Leopard: I don't believe you.

Turtle: It's true. And it's bigger than yours, too. In fact, his drum is so big that Ruler can get inside of it and hide.

Leopard: What's so great about that? I can hide in my drum too. See?

Narrator 1: Leopard climbed into his drum just like Turtle had hoped. Then, Turtle stuffed a big pot that he had brought with him into the opening of the drum.

Leopard: Hey! What are you doing? Let me out of here!

Narrator 2: Turtle didn't answer. He tied a rope around the drum and slowly began to pull it.

Narrator 1: Leopard was furious. He begged Turtle to let him out.

Turtle: If I let you out, will you give Ruler of the Sky your drum?

Leopard: Yes, yes. He can have my drum. Just let me out of this small space. It's hard for me to breathe in here.

Turtle: And will you promise to go away and not bother us any more?

Leopard: Yes, I promise. Now get me out of here. And be quick about it!

Narrator 2: Turtle took away the pot. Leopard jumped out and ran off into the jungle.

Narrator 1: When Turtle gave the drum to Ruler of the Sky, Ruler was *very* happy.

Ruler: Thank you, Turtle. You have given me something that no one else could. Now I want to return the favor and give you something. What would you like to have? Name it, and it's yours.

Turtle: Well, all of the animals have something that will protect them when they are in danger. But I have nothing. Could you give me something that will make me safe, too?

Narrator 2: Immediately Ruler of the Sky used his magical powers and granted Turtle's wish.

Narrator 1: And to this day, all turtles carry a hard shell on their back, which protects them from harm.

Why Rattlesnake Has Fangs

Summary

Soft Child, the snake, was gentle and other animals teased him about his rattle. Sun God felt sorry for him and provided protection for the snake. This is a Pima tale. RL3

Presentation Suggestions

Both narrators could stand together off to one side. The other characters could be arranged across the stage in order of appearance: Deer, Soft Child, Squirrel, Bird, Fox, Bear, Rabbit, and Sun God. When Sun God reads, he could move and stand next to Soft Child.

Props

The animals could wear something symbolic of what they are: antlers for the deer, bushy tail for the squirrel and fox, feathers for the bird, short tails for the rabbit and bear. Sun God could wear yellow. Soft Child could hold and shake a rattle, and perhaps insert fake fangs into his mouth when he acquires them.

Delivery

Voices should vary according to the size of the animals. Bear should have the deepest voice, and the bird should have a higher pitched voice. Sun God's voice should be warm and smooth. Soft Child should attempt to draw out any words that have an "s" in them. Rabbit should sound a little mean.

Related Books

Arnosky, Jim. *All About Rattlesnakes*. New York: Scholastic, 1997.
Berman, Ruth. *Buzzing Rattlesnakes*. Minneapolis, MN: Lerner Publications, 1998.
McDonald, Mary Ann. *Rattlesnakes*. Minneapolis, MN: Capstone Press, 1996.
Noble, Trinka Hakes. *Jimmy's Boa Bounces Back*. New York: Dial Books, 1984.
Stone, Lynn M. *Secret Lives of Snakes*. Vero Beach, FL: Rourke Book Co., 2001.

Characters

Narrator 1
Narrator 2

Deer

Soft Child

Squirrel

Bird

Fox

Bear

Rabbit

Sun God

Why Rattlesnake Has Fangs

Narrator 1: What do you think of when you hear the word "rattlesnake"?

Narrator 2: Do you think of a mean snake that rattles its tail before it strikes and hurts you?

Narrator 1: If that's what you think, you're partly right.

Narrator 2: The rattlesnake used to be a gentle little animal, not at all mean. The Sun God and other animals called him Soft Child.

Deer: Soft Child, you are nice, but not very smart. What would you do if someone attacked you?

Soft Child: I never thought about that.

Squirrel: If someone tried to attack me, I'd run as fast as I could up a tree.

Deer: And I'd knock him over with my antlers.

Soft Child: I guess I'd talk to him and find out why he wanted to get me.

Deer: That's your problem, Soft Child. You're too nice.

Bird: Hello, friends. Look up! I'm in my nest, and I can hear you talking. I think the problem with Soft Child is that Sun God forgot to give him something to use for protection. All he has is a rattle, and that sure doesn't scare anyone.

Narrator 1: Bird was right. The animals weren't scared when they heard Soft Child's rattle. In fact, they liked to hear it and had fun dancing to the sounds it made.

Narrator 2: Although they liked to hear the rattle, they all teased the snake.

Fox: Shake, Soft Child, shake!

Bear: Shake your tail faster, Soft Child.

Narrator 1: One day, at a ceremonial dance, a mean rabbit wanted to have some fun with the snake.

Rabbit: Here's what we'll do. I'll throw Soft Child to you, Deer. You toss him to someone else. We'll throw him around like a ball. Let's see what he does.

Narrator 2: The animals had a good time tossing the snake around. Soft Child didn't like it at all. But there was nothing he could do to stop them.

Narrator 1: Sun God saw what was happening and felt sorry for Soft Child.

Narrator 2: After a while, the animals got tired of throwing the snake around. They put him on the ground and left him alone.

Sun God: Soft Child, I'm sorry I didn't give you something that would protect you from harm. To make up for that I want you to get two sharp thorns from the devil's claw plant. Put them in the upper jaw of your mouth.

Narrator 1: Soft Child did as he was told. When he had the two sharp thorns in his upper jaw, Sun God spoke to him.

Sun God: Now you have something that will hurt others when you have to defend yourself. But before you strike, use your rattle as a warning. And strike only when you have to.

Narrator 2: The next day, Rabbit saw the snake and went up to him.

Rabbit: Well, well, well. If it isn't Soft Child, my favorite toy. I feel like seeing how far I can throw you.

Narrator 1: As the rabbit got near the snake, Soft Child shook his rattle as a warning.

Rabbit: Hah! Are you trying to scare me with your rattle? Sorry, it won't work! Instead of throwing you, I'll see how far I can kick you!

Narrator 2: The rabbit lifted a foot and was ready to kick the snake, when Soft Child used his thorns on Rabbit.

Rabbit: *OWWW!* That hurt! I'm not messing around with you!

Narrator 1: Rabbit ran away in pain. When the other animals saw what had happened, they backed away from the snake.

Narrator 2: After that, the snake wasn't called Soft Child anymore.

Narrator 1: To this day, the rattlesnake only strikes when it has to.

Narrator 2: And, when everyone hears its rattle, they are afraid.

Why the Crab's Eyes Are on Stalks

Summary

Scales cover crab's eyes, and he can't see. He makes his way to the water, which washes away the scales. However, from trying so hard to see, his eyes have popped out on stalks. This is a Seneca tale. RL2

Presentation Suggestions

Because there are so few characters, the narrators should stand together, with the crab close by.

Props

Perhaps large eyes could be drawn and pasted on the end of two sticks. Crab could pick them up and hold them when the narrators conclude the story.

Delivery

Through pacing, Crab could show his emotions. Slow at first, when he is enjoying the sun, then getting faster to show his anxiety over being unable to see.

Related Books

Greenaway, Theresa. *The Secret World of Crabs.* Austin, TX: Greentree Steck-Vaughn, 2001.
Kipling, Rudyard. *The Crab That Played with the Sea.* New York: HarperCollins, 1983.
Knutson, Barbara. *Why the Crab Has No Head.* Minneapolis, MN: Carolrhoda Books, 1987.
McClung, Robert M. *Horseshoe Crab.* New York: Morrow Jr. Books, 1967.

Characters

Narrator 1
Narrator 2
Crab

Why the Crab's Eyes Are on Stalks

Narrator 1: One warm, sunny day, crab came out from the water.

Narrator 2: He was walking sideways just like he always did.

Crab: The sun feels warm and good on my wet body. I think I'll stay here for a little while and soak up the rays of the sun.

Narrator 1: Crab felt so rested that he soon fell asleep. He began to dry up from the heat of the sun.

Narrator 2: Scales formed over his eyes, and when he woke up, Crab couldn't see.

Crab: Why is it so dark? Where did the sun go? I can't see anything!

Narrator 1: Then he realized what had happened.

Crab: Something is covering my eyes! I was in the sun too long. I must get back into the water.

Narrator 2: Crab ran, hoping he was heading for the water. Because he couldn't see, he bumped into a tree.

Crab: Ouch! What is this? I can feel roots of a tree. I think it's an oak tree. Somehow I got to the top of the mountain where the oak trees grow.

Narrator 1: Crab turned in a different direction and soon bumped into another tree. He felt its roots.

Crab: These are the roots of a maple tree. They grow part way down the mountain. Good, I must be getting closer to the water.

Narrator 2: Crab made his way down the mountain until he bumped into another tree. As he did before, he felt the roots.

Crab: This is an elm tree. It grows near the bottom of the mountain. Now I know I'm heading toward the water.

Narrator 1: A short distance later, Crab bumped into a willow tree.

Crab: Great! Willow trees grow next to the water.

Narrator 2: Crab sniffed.

Crab: Yes! I can smell water.

Narrator 1: Crab went into the water and soon the scales dropped off from his eyes.

Narrator 2: Because Crab tried so hard to see while he was running, his eyes had popped out on stalks. And to this day, all crabs have eyes on stalks.

Why the Sun and the Moon Are in the Sky

Summary

When Sun wanted to visit his friend, Water, he always had to go to Water's home. To accommodate Water and all of his people, Sun built a large house. But as Water's people filled the house, Sun and his wife, Moon, were forced out. This is a myth of the Efik people of Southern Nigeria. RL3

Presentation Suggestions

Both narrators could stand to one side of the stage. Water, Sun, and Moon could be in the center.

Props

The stage area could be decorated with pictures of various sea fish and animals. Sun could wear yellow, Water could wear blue, and Moon could wear white or pale yellow.

Delivery

Water's voice should be the loudest of all the voices, while Moon should have the softest voice.

Related Books

Asch, Frank. *The Sun Is My Favorite Star.* San Diego, CA: Gulliver Books, 2000.
Branley, Franklyn M. *What the Moon Is Like.* New York: HarperCollins, 2000.
Dayrell, Elphinstone. *Why the Sun and Moon Live in the Sky.* Boston: Houghton Mifflin, 1968.

Characters

Narrator 1
Narrator 2
Sun
Water
Moon

Why the Sun and the Moon Are in the Sky

Narrator 1: Many years ago, Sun lived on earth and was good friends with Water.

Narrator 2: Sun always went to Water's home to visit, but Water never went to Sun's home.

Sun: Why don't you ever come to see me, Water? If I want to see you, I always have to go to your home.

Water: Dear friend, I would love to go to your home to visit. However, your home isn't big enough. You see, if I came, I'd have to bring my people with me, and you don't have enough room for all of us. We would push you out.

Sun: Who are your people, and how many are you talking about?

Water: Hundreds. Perhaps thousands. First, there are all of the fish, big and small. Then, the lobsters, and crabs, and oysters, and so many other creatures that I can't begin to name them all.

Sun: I get the picture. You do have a lot of people, don't you?

Water: Yes. And if you *really* want me and my people to come visit you, you'll have to build a bigger house—a *tremendous* house.

Sun: Then that's what I'll do!

Narrator 1: Sun returned home to his wife, Moon, and told her of his visit with Water.

Sun: We're going to build a bigger home so my friend, Water, will be able to visit us.

Moon: That's fine with me. Lately I've wanted a bigger home, but I didn't want to bother you about it. Let's get to work!

Narrator 2: Sun, with the help of Moon, worked hard and built a lovely, great big enormous enclosure. He was sure it would hold Water. When it was finished, Sun went to Water.

Sun: Well, Water, now I have a *very* big home, and again I invite you to come visit.

Water: Thank you, Sun, for making it possible for me to come to visit you. It was good of you to build a larger home, and my people and I will come to you shortly.

Narrator 1: Water and all of his people soon arrived at Sun's house.

Water: Sun, your home is definitely big, but will it be safe for all of us to enter?

Sun: Of course it is. Please come in.

Narrator 2: Sun was delighted that his friend was finally visiting him. He watched Water enter, along with whales, dolphins, sharks, some fish, and water animals.

Narrator 1: Soon the water was knee deep.

Narrator 2: When Water saw that only a few of his people were in Sun's home, he called to Sun.

Water: Not all of my people are in. Is it still safe for others to join us?

Sun: Yes indeed. There's plenty of room. Bring in more of your people.

Narrator 1: Water flowed in with new fish, crabs, lobsters, and other water people. Now the water was neck-high.

Narrator 2: Again, Water called to Sun.

Water: There are still some of my people here that need to go into your home. Is it still safe? Shall I keep coming?

Narrator 1: Sun and Moon looked at the water surrounding them. They both answered.

Sun and Moon: Yes, please come.

Narrator 2: Water poured in with more of his people.

Water: Am I pushing you out? Is it all right for me to come in?

Narrator 2: Moon was concerned.

Moon: Oh dear, now what do we do?

Sun: We'll have to move to the roof.

Narrator 1: They told Water to come, and Water continued to rush in with more fish and sea animals, until the roof was covered.

Moon: Water has taken over our house! There's no more room for us!

Sun: I'm afraid we'll have to leave our house and earth.

Moon: Where will we go?

Narrator 2: Sun looked up.

Sun: We'll move to the sky.

Narrator 1: And that's what they did.

Narrator 2: Ever since then, Sun and Moon have lived in the sky.

How the Milky Way Came to Be

Summary

A greedy man steals straw and escapes to the sky, leaving a path behind him. This is a story that is told in Persia and Africa. RL3

Presentation Suggestions

Because there are so few characters, consider having them close together, with the man a few feet away from the two narrators.

Props

You may want to have a pile of straw at one side of the stage for effect.

Delivery

The man's voice should be distinct—perhaps sly-sounding with a slight snarl.

Related Books

Bruchac, Joseph. *The Story of the Milky Way: A Cherokee Tale*. New York: Dial Books, 1995.
Lee, Jeanne M. *The Legend of the Milky Way*. New York: Henry Holt & Co., 1982.
Oughton, Jerrie. *How the Stars Fell into the Sky*. Boston: Houghton Mifflin, 1992.
Shaw, Charles Green. *It Looked Like Spilt Milk*. New York: HarperCollins, 1972.

Characters

Narrator 1
Narrator 2
Man

How the Milky Way Came to Be

Narrator 1: Have you ever looked up to the sky and noticed millions of stars so close together that they look like a white path? That's called the Milky Way.

Narrator 2: Now you're probably wondering why it's called the Milky Way, and how the stars got so close together. You're about to find out.

Narrator 1: Many, many years ago, there was a mean and greedy man.

Narrator 2: He was also sly. He never worked, so he never bought what he needed. Instead, he took things from others.

Man: My horse is getting old and can't pull my wagon for long trips anymore. I need a new horse.

Narrator 1: So on a dark, moonless night, the man went to a nearby farm and exchanged his horse for one that was in the field. Of course, no one saw him, and he went home with a new horse.

Narrator 2: Another time, the greedy man needed meat.

Man: I want lamb for dinner. And I can use the lamb's wool and skin to make a blanket and maybe a hat and gloves. I noticed sheep grazing in a pasture not far from here. I'm certain the farmer won't notice if one is missing.

Narrator 1: When it was dark, and he was certain that no one could see him, the man grabbed a lamb from the pasture and took it home.

Narrator 2: One day, the man needed straw, and since he didn't have any in his own field, he decided to help himself to his neighbor's.

Man: This is the perfect night. There is no moon, and no stars to shed light. No one will see me.

Narrator 1: He hitched his new horse to a wagon, crept into his neighbor's field, and began to load up his cart with straw.

Man: Whew, I didn't realize what hard work this would be. My arms are getting tired, and my back hurts. I'll rest a little and work slower.

Narrator 2: But because the man did rest and slow down so often, he saw the sun rise just as he finished.

Man: Oh dear, it's morning. People will be waking up, and someone is certain to see me. I must hide my load of straw so no one will see it. But where can I go?

Narrator 1: He looked to his right and left.

Man: There's nothing around but open fields. No place to hide my wagon.

Narrator 2: He looked in front and behind him, and again saw nothing but open fields.

Narrator 1: Then he looked up.

Man: Ah! The sky would be a perfect place for me to hide my wagon of straw. It is wide and empty. No one is there at all.

Narrator 2: The man climbed into the front of his wagon, snapped the reins, and called to his horse.

Man: Let's go! Up, up, and away.

Narrator 1: Soon he was sailing across the middle of the sky.

Man: Faster, faster horse. No one must see us.

Narrator 2: All day, the man drove his wagon across the sky, picking up speed as he went. At the end of the day, when the sun settled behind the hills of the earth, the man and his stolen straw had disappeared.

Narrator 1: But in his hurry, the man hadn't noticed that some of the straw had dropped out of his wagon.

Narrator 2: The fallen straw showed the path he had taken.

Narrator 1: Now, on a clear night, when you look up, you'll see a path in the sky—a path made of shining straw that we call the Milky Way.

Narrator 2: You probably won't be able to find the greedy, sly man, but you'll know which way he went.

Why the Sea Is Salt

Summary

A sea captain obtains a magic mill and orders it to grind salt. He can't make the self-grinding mill stop and eventually, the weight of the salt sinks his ship. Although this tale is known across northern Europe, as well as Japan, this rendition comes from Norway. There are many other stories from different countries that explain why the sea is salt. RL3

Presentation Suggestions

The narrators should stand on opposite sides of the stage. Across the front of the stage, in staggered form, the other characters could stand in the following order: Martin, Jack, Old Man, Hilda, Hill Man, and Skipper. As Jack interacts with the various characters, he could either move closer to them, or step forward when he speaks. The characters to whom he speaks could also step forward.

Props

If possible, have a small mill that could be passed to the characters as they use it. Martin should be dressed in nice clothes, while Jack should look poorly dressed. The old man could have a long, white beard (paper or cotton). Hilda could wear a kerchief on her head. The skipper could wear a sailor captain's hat.

Delivery

The old man should have a soft, shaky voice. The other characters should develop voices that would be appropriate to what they're saying.

Related Books

Bat-Ami, Miriam. *Sea, Salt, and Air.* New York: Simon & Schuster, 1998.
Hamilton, Kersten. *This Is the Ocean.* Honesdale, PA: Boyds Mills Press, 2001.
Leach, Maria. *How the People Sang the Mountains Up.* New York: Viking Press, 1967.

Characters

Narrator 1
Narrator 2

Jack (the poor brother)
Martin (the rich brother)
Old Man
Hill Man
Hilda (Jack's wife)
Skipper

Why the Sea Is Salt

Narrator 1: A long time ago, there were two brothers: Martin, who was rich, and Jack, who was poor.

Narrator 2: One Christmas Eve, Jack, the poor brother, had no food in the house. Not even a crumb of bread! So he went to his brother, Martin.

Jack: Martin, I'm embarrassed to come to you for help, but I have no choice. It's Christmas Eve, and I have no food for my family or me. Would you be good enough to give us some food so that we may celebrate Christmas?

Martin: What do you mean you have *no* food? Surely you have something to eat.

Jack: No, we have nothing. No meat, no fruits or vegetables, not even a cracker or piece of bread.

Narrator 1: Now, this was not the first time Jack had come to Martin for help.

Narrator 2: Martin was stingy and didn't like to give anything away. However, Jack was his brother and he felt he must help him—again.

Martin: Very well, Jack. I'll give you a whole piece of bacon, a few potatoes, and two loaves of bread for you and your family. I'll even give you some candles. But, this is the last time I'll help you. So don't ever come to me again!

Jack: I promise, Martin. I will never set foot in your house from this day on. Thank you for your help.

Narrator 1: As Jack headed home, he met an old man with a white beard. The old man looked very thin and tired, and he had a hungry look about him.

Narrator 2: The old man stretched out his hand to Jack and spoke to him in a soft, shaky voice.

Old Man: Please, kind sir, will you give a poor old man something to eat?

Jack: I know how you must feel. I, too, have been begging for food. But I'm not so poor that I can't give you something on this Christmas Eve.

Narrator 1: Jack handed the old man a candle and a loaf of bread. He was getting ready to cut off a piece from the bacon when the old man stopped him.

Old Man: I don't need any more. You've given me enough for now, and the loaf of bread will provide me with food for several days. In return for your kindness, I want to tell you about something very special.

Narrator 2: Jack moved closer to the old man so he could hear what he had to say.

Old Man: Nearby, you will find an entrance to the home of the folks who live underground. They have a mill, which can grind out anything they want except bacon. You must get inside their underground home.

Jack: Why? I don't understand.

Old Man: Don't interrupt me! I was about to tell you when you interrupted.

Jack: Sorry!

Old Man: When you get inside, they will want to buy your bacon. But don't sell it to them. Instead, tell them you'll trade it for the mill that stands behind their door. And when you come out with the mill, I'll show you how to handle it.

Narrator 1: Jack thanked the old man for his advice and followed his directions to the home of the underground folks.

Narrator 2: For a while, Jack stood outside the cave. Then he went inside. Everything was just as the old man had said. As soon as they saw Jack with his bacon, the underground people gathered around him, making offers to buy it.

Jack: Really, now, I'd like to sell this bacon to you, but my wife and family are looking forward to having it for our Christmas dinner. I don't want to disappoint them.

Hill Man: I'll give you so much money that you could buy ten times the amount of bacon that you have now.

Jack: I can see that you all have your hearts set on having this bacon, so I guess I should let you have it. But, instead of taking your money, I'm willing to exchange my bacon for that handsome mill you have behind the door.

Hill Man: No! That is out of the question.

Narrator 1: They haggled back and forth. Jack stuck to what he had said, and at last, the hill folk gave up their mill for the bacon.

Narrator 2: Jack took the mill and left the cave. He went into the woods, where he met the old man.

Jack: Here's the mill! Now show me how to handle it.

Narrator 1: After he learned how to use it, Jack thanked the old man and hurried home.

Narrator 2: He reached his home just as the clock struck twelve on Christmas Eve. His wife, Hilda, was waiting for him. She was *very* angry!

Hilda: Where in the world have you been? I've been waiting and watching for you all night.

Jack: I'm sorry, but I couldn't get back any sooner. I had to go a long way to get something, and I can assure you, it is well worth the wait. Let me show you.

Narrator 1: Jack put the mill on the table and told it to grind lights, then a tablecloth, then meat, then ale, and so on until they had everything they wanted for a fine Christmas dinner.

Hilda: I don't believe my eyes! You only said one word, and the mill ground out whatever you wanted. That's remarkable! Where did you find such a wonderful mill?

Jack: I can't tell you, Hilda. And it really doesn't matter where it came from. What does matter is that it's a good one, and the mill stream will *never* stop.

Narrator 2: For the next several days, the mill ground out wonderful things to eat, which Jack and his family enjoyed. Then, Jack had an idea.

Jack: Let's invite our friends and family to a great feast, which the mill will provide.

Narrator 1: Of course, Martin was invited, and when he saw all that was on the table, as well as what was in the cupboards, the rich brother grew wild with anger. He didn't think Jack should have anything.

Martin: How could it be that only a few nights ago, on Christmas Eve, you came to me, begging for food because you had nothing to eat. And now, you have more than enough. Where did you get all this wealth?

Jack: From this mill that is behind the door. I'll show you.

Narrator 2: As Martin watched Jack make the mill grind all kinds of things, he decided that he wanted the mill. They discussed it and finally came to an agreement.

Jack: I'll give you the mill at hay-harvest time, at which time you will pay me three hundred dollars for it. Meanwhile, I will continue to use it.

Narrator 1: Over the next few months, Jack made the mill grind meat and drink, as well as gold that would last for years.

Narrator 2: When hay-harvest time came, Jack turned the mill over to his brother for three hundred dollars. Martin was in such a hurry to take the mill home and make it grind things that he forgot to learn how to handle it.

Narrator 1: The next day, Martin told his wife to leave the house. He would stay home and prepare dinner. When the time came, Martin put the mill on the kitchen table and told it to grind herrings and broth.

Narrator 2: The mill set to work. First, all of the dishes were filled. Then all of the tubs filled, and so on, until the kitchen floor was covered with herrings and broth.

Narrator 1: Martin yelled at the mill to make it stop. He twisted and turned the mill and did everything he could think of. But the mill continued to grind until the entire house was filled with herrings and broth.

Narrator 2: Martin opened the front door to escape and was swept from the house in a stream of herrings and broth. Whoever he met along the road, he yelled to them.

Martin: Eat! Drink! As much as you want! But be careful that you don't drown in the broth.

Narrator 1: Martin ran to his brother's house, and begged him to take back the mill. Jack took it back, and soon the mill stopped grinding herrings and broth.

Narrator 2: By now, Jack lived in a fine house near the sea. He ground so much gold that he covered his house with it. Everyone who sailed past his house saw the gold gleam and glisten, and knew about the wonderful mill that could grind anything.

Narrator 1: One day, the skipper of a ship decided to stop by Jack's house to see the mill for himself.

Skipper: I understand your mill can grind anything you want it to. Can it grind salt?

Jack: I'm sure it could. After all, it can grind anything.

Skipper: If it can grind salt, then I must have the mill. It would save me from taking so many long and dangerous voyages to find salt.

Narrator 2: They struck a deal, and the skipper went off with the mill. But he hurried away so fast that he hadn't asked Jack how to handle it.

Narrator 1: The skipper returned to his ship and set sail. When he was far out to sea, he brought the mill on deck.

Skipper: Grind salt, mill, and grind it good and fast.

Narrator 2: Immediately, the mill began to grind salt. It ground so fast that the ship soon filled with salt.

Skipper: Stop grinding, mill.

Narrator 1: But the mill didn't stop. No matter what the skipper said or did, the mill continued to grind. The pile of salt grew higher and higher until eventually the ship sank.

Narrator 2: Of course, the mill was never stopped, so to this very day, it is still grinding away. And that is why the sea is salt.

Why the Big Dipper Is in the Sky

Summary

A young girl enters the woods one hot summer night, searching for water for her thirsty mother. Because of her kindness to a stray dog and an old man, the tin dipper she carries eventually becomes diamonds, which go to the sky. This is an American folktale. RL4

Presentation Suggestions

Both narrators could stand together to one side of the stage. Mother and Abby should be in the center of the stage area. The dog and old man should stand on the other side of Abby.

Props

Perhaps Abby could wear a nightgown and hold a dipper (ladle) in her hand. Mother could wear a nightcap. The old man could hold a walking stick, and the dog could have a tail pinned to its backside.

Delivery

In the beginning, Mother's voice should sound slightly raspy from thirst, but after she gets her water, she can use a normal voice. Abby's voice should show her caring and sweet nature. If possible, the old man could have an elderly, shaky quality.

Related Books

Branley, Franklyn M. *The Big Dipper*. New York: Thomas Y. Crowell, 1962.
Rosen, Sydney. *Where's the Big Dipper?* Minneapolis, MN: Carolrhoda Books, 1995.
Wandelmaier, Roy. *Stars*. Mahwah, NJ: Troll Books, 1985.

Characters

Narrator 1

Narrator 2

Abby

Mother
Dog
Old Man

Why the Big Dipper Is in the Sky

Narrator 1: Once, a very long time ago, there was a girl named Abby who lived with her mother in a small cabin. Her father had died when Abby was a baby.

Narrator 2: Abby and her mother always took care of each other, and did everything together.

Narrator 1: One unusually hot summer evening, Abby couldn't fall asleep. She tossed and turned, trying to get comfortable, but nothing helped.

Narrator 2: You see, this was so long ago that it was before air conditioning was invented.

Abby: I feel miserable. There isn't even a breeze to make me cool.

Narrator 1: In the bedroom next to her, Abby could hear her mother moaning as she, too, tossed and turned.

Mother: Water! I need water! I'm so thirsty.

Narrator 2: Abby knew that her mother had not been feeling well all day and probably had a temperature. A drink of water might cool her and make her feel better. So Abby went into her mother's room.

Abby: Momma, would you like me to go to the well and get you a fresh drink of water?

Mother: Oh, yes! I would appreciate that, dear. Thank you.

Narrator 1: Abby went into the kitchen, removed the tin dipper from a hook on the wall, and headed for the well.

Narrator 2: In that time, there was no electricity or running water, either.

Narrator 1: When Abby reached the well, she dropped the bucket down, then pulled it back up. She put the dipper into the bucket, but the bucket was empty.

Abby: Oh dear! It's been so hot that the well has dried up. Now I have no water for my mother. What should I do?

Narrator 2: Suddenly, she remembered something.

Abby: There's a lovely spring in the woods that has clear, cold water. I'll ask Momma to let me get water for her from the spring.

Narrator 1: Abby ran home and into her mother's bedroom.

Abby: Momma, the well has dried up, but if you'd like, I'll go to the spring in the woods and get you some cold water.

Mother: I must have a drink of water, Abby. If you don't mind going into the woods at night, I would be grateful. But please be careful. I wouldn't want anything to happen to you.

Narrator 2: Abby put on her slippers and headed for the woods, holding the tin dipper in her hand.

Narrator 1: When she reached the edge of the woods, Abby stopped.

Abby: It's very dark in there. Maybe I'd better not go in after all. But then I won't be able to get Momma the water she needs.

Narrator 2: Bravely, Abby stepped into the woods determined to help her mother. As her eyes grew accustomed to the dark, she walked a little faster.

Narrator 1: Her nightgown caught on branches, and she stumbled on rocks and roots that were on the path. But still she walked on.

Narrator 2: After a while, she stopped to listen for the sounds of the spring.

Abby: I don't hear anything that sounds like running water. Maybe I took a wrong turn. Or perhaps the spring has dried up.

Narrator 1: She walked a little farther and stopped again.

Abby: I hear it! The spring is nearby.

Narrator 2: She followed the sound of the running water until she came to the spring. Abby put the dipper into the spring and filled it with water. Then she turned around and headed for home.

Narrator 1: She hadn't gone very far when a stray dog came out from the woods. Its tongue was hanging out of its mouth, and it was panting.

Dog: *(panting sounds)*

Abby: You poor little dog. You must be very thirsty.

Narrator 2: She poured some of the water from the dipper into her hand and offered it to the dog. The dog lapped up every drop.

Narrator 1: Then the dog gave two sharp barks.

Dog: Arf! Arf!

Narrator 2: It was as if the dog was saying "thank you". Immediately, the dog ran off, allowing Abby to continue her journey home.

Narrator 1: As she walked, she noticed that the woods weren't as dark as they had been when she entered. She looked up to the sky.

Abby: That's strange. There's no moon or stars in the sky, yet it's brighter now and I can easily see.

Narrator 2: She noticed that the light seemed to be coming from her hand.

Narrator 1: When she looked at her hand, she saw that the dipper was no longer tin. It was now silver, just like a full moon.

Narrator 2: Now that it was brighter, Abby walked faster, careful not to spill any of the water in her dipper. Suddenly, an old man appeared in front of her.

Old Man: Please, dear child, would you tell me where I could get a drink of cold water? I've been walking all day in this terrible heat. All of the brooks are dry and I can't find a spring. I'm tired and very thirsty.

Abby: If you continue on this path, you'll come to a fine spring. Meanwhile, drink some of the water I have in this dipper.

Narrator 1: The old man took a few sips.

Old Man: Thank you, my child. I'm grateful to you. Now I will go to the spring you told me about.

Narrator 2: The old man left, and once again, Abby headed for home. She noticed that now it was lighter than it was before, and looked down at the dipper she held. It was no longer silver, but had turned to gold, like the golden sun.

Narrator 1: Abby could see much better now, so she walked faster until she reached her home. She ran into her mother's bedroom and gave her the water, which she gulped down.

Mother: I can't remember when I've ever been so thirsty. Thank you, Abby, for bringing water to me. I feel much better now. Put the dipper in the corner of the room and sit by my side. We'll talk for a while.

Narrator 2: Abby did as she was told, and while they talked, they noticed strange, bright lights flashing on the walls of the room.

Abby: Look, Momma, the lights are coming from the dipper. It's changed into sparkling diamonds!

Narrator 1: As they both looked at the dipper, the diamonds traveled across the wall, then went out the window and rose into the sky.

Narrator 2: There they turned into seven bright twinkling stars in the form of a big dipper.

Narrator 1: As we told you in the beginning, Abby and her mother lived many years ago, but if you look up into the sky some bright, starry night, you'll see that the big dipper is still there.

Narrator 2: And when you see it, think of Abby, the girl who was brave enough to go into the dark woods alone to get her mother a drink of water.

How the Rainbow Was Made

Summary

When Sun and Rain argue over which is more important, Mother Nature separates them. They each discover that they are both important and return home. Mother Nature is pleased and gives a gift to the world. This is based on a Native American Indian legend. RL5

Presentation Suggestions

The narrators could be separated and stand on opposite sides of the stage. Mother Nature, Sun, and Rain should be grouped together in the beginning. Sun and Rain can walk to opposite sides of the stage when the narrator reads about their departures. They can read their lines from the sides, then return to center when the narrator tells of their return home. Mother Nature would remain in the center.

Props

Sun could wear yellow, Rain could wear light blue, and Mother Nature could wear brown. Consider having premade bands depicting each color of the rainbow, and fixing them to a wall or board with Velcro as the narrator says the colors.

Delivery

Sun's voice should be soft and warm, while Rain could have a crisp voice. Mother Nature should sound "motherly," and convey her feelings of annoyance and pride when appropriate.

Related Books

Asch, Frank. *Skyfire*. New York: Simon & Schuster, 1988.

Craft, Ruth. *The Day of the Rainbow*. New York: Viking Press, 1989.

Freeman, Don. *A Rainbow of My Own*. New York: Puffin, 1978.

Robbins, Ruth. *How the First Rainbow Was Made*. Boston: Houghton Mifflin, 1980.

Rupprecht, Siegfried P. *The Tale of the Vanishing Rainbow*. New York: North-South Books, 1989.

Characters

Narrator 1
Narrator 2
Sun
Rain
Mother Nature

How the Rainbow Was Made

Narrator 1: Mother Nature was on her hands and knees, busy preparing for spring.

Narrator 2: While she worked, her two children, Sun and Rain, were behind her, arguing over which one was better and more important.

Sun: Dear brother Rain, I am truly better than you. I bring warmth to the world, and without me nothing would grow.

Rain: What are you talking about? I am *much* more important than you. If it weren't for me, the world wouldn't have water. My water is what helps plants grow.

Narrator 1: They continued to argue, and as they did, their voices grew louder and louder.

Narrator 2: After a while, Mother Nature couldn't take their bickering any longer.

Mother Nature: Stop it this minute! I can't stand to hear you argue and yell at each other over which one is more important. I think you need to be separated. Get away from each other for a while.

Narrator 1: She pointed to the east.

Mother Nature: Sun, I want you to go to the end of the world *that* way.

Narrator 2: Then she pointed to the west.

Mother Nature: And Rain, you go to the end of the world *that* way. And I don't want either of you to return home until you are ready to accept each other and get along.

Narrator 1: Although they argued, Sun and Rain really loved each other and didn't want to be separated.

Narrator 2: But they each thought this might be a chance to see who really was more important.

Narrator 1: So, Sun headed toward the east. When she reached the end of the world, she smiled.

Sun: Hmmm, this is nice.

Narrator 2: Her smile warmed the earth and made seeds that were hiding under the ground pop up, and begin to grow.

Sun: I was right. I *can* make things grow.

Narrator 1: Sun smiled a little broader, and soon flowers burst open.

Sun: Such beautiful flowers. I see so many colors—red, yellow, white, and pink. I wonder what will happen if I smile stronger.

Narrator 2: Her wider smile made leaves on the trees turn bright green, and the grass looked like a plush, green carpet.

Sun: Look at all I have done because of my warm smile!

Narrator 1: Sun sent out stronger beams, but then, something terrible happened.

Narrator 2: The flowers wilted. The green leaves turned brown and fell from the trees. The grass was no longer green. The water in the ponds, creeks, streams, and lakes evaporated, leaving only dry, cracked beds.

Narrator 1: When Sun saw what she had done, she was very upset.

Sun: Oh dear, I guess my warm smile is too much. The plants need Rain, too.

Narrator 2: Meanwhile, Rain had journeyed to the west, and when he reached the end of the world, he began to drizzle.

Narrator 1: As soon as Rain's water hit the earth, the seeds that were hiding below began to grow.

Rain: See that! I was right! I make things grow. I'll help these seeds along with a little more water.

Narrator 2: Flowers appeared and burst open in every color you could imagine.

Rain: I knew it! I'm more important than Sun, and these flowers prove it.

Narrator 1: Rain fell a little harder, and soon the grass and the leaves on trees became bright green.

Rain: This is great! I've created a beautiful world. I'll let more water fall.

Narrator 2: Rain fell harder and harder, until something terrible happened.

Narrator 1: The ponds, creeks, streams, and lakes filled with water and overflowed their banks.

Narrator 2: The water drowned the grass and flowers, and the leaves on the trees got sick and fell to the ground.

Narrator 1: When Rain saw what he had done, he felt very bad.

Rain: I now see that I'm not enough. Sun is important, too.

Narrator 2: Now that Sun and Rain realized that both of them were important to the world, they returned home and told their mother what they had learned.

Mother Nature: I'm proud of you, children, and I want to let everyone know how important you both are. I'll give the world a special gift.

Narrator 1: Mother Nature took out her paints, and with one stroke of a brush, painted a big red arc in the sky.

Narrator 2: Under the red arc, she painted an orange one, followed quickly by a yellow arc.

Narrator 1: Next came a green arc, then blue, and finally, indigo.

Narrator 2: Mother Nature was pleased with her work.

Mother Nature: I'll call this a rainbow.

Narrator 1: So, every time you see a rainbow in the sky, you'll know that Sun and Rain are getting along and respect each other.

Narrator 2: And you'll also know that neither Sun nor Rain is better—they are both important to the world.

Resources

Books about Readers Theatre

Bauer, Caroline Feller. 1987. *Presenting Reader's Theater: Plays and Poems to Read Aloud*. Bronx, NY: H. W. Wilson Company, 1987.

———. 1992. *Read for the Fun of It: Active Programming with Books for Children*. Bronx, NY: H. W. Wilson Company, 1992.

Coger, L. I., and M. R. White. *Readers Theatre Handbook: A Dramatic Approach to Literature*. Glenview, IL: Scott Foresman, 1982.

Kaye, Marvin. *Readers Theatre: What It Is and How to Stage It*. United Kingdom: Fantasy Fiction Co., 1995.

Raczuk, Helen, and Marilyn Smith. *Invitation to Readers Theatre: Grades K–6*. Spruce Grove, Alberta, Canada: U-Otter-Read-It, 1997.

Ratliff, Gerald Lee. *Introduction to Readers Theatre: A Guide to Classroom Performance*. Colorado Springs, CO: Meriwether Publishing, 1999.

Sloyer, S. *Readers Theatre: Story Dramatization in the Classroom*. Urbana, IL: National Council for Teachers of English, 1982.

Sources for Readers Theatre Scripts

Barchers, Suzanne. *Fifty Fabulous Fables: Beginning Readers Theatre*. Englewood, CO: Teacher Ideas Press, 1997.

———. *Readers Theatre for Beginning Readers*. Englewood, CO: Teacher Ideas Press, 1993.

Blau, Lisa. *Fall Is Fabulous!: Readers Theatre Scripts and Extended Activities*. Bellevue, WA: One From the Heart, 1997.

Criscoe, B. L., and P. J. Lanasa. *Fairy Tales for Two Readers*. Englewood, CO: Teacher Ideas Press, 1995.

Fredericks, A. D. *Frantic Frogs and Other Frankly Fractured Folktales for Readers Theatre*. Englewood, CO: Teacher Ideas Press, 1993.

———. *Tadpole Tales and Other Totally Terrific Treats for Readers Theatre*. Englewood, CO: Teacher Ideas Press, 1997.

Georges, C., and C. Cornett. *Reader's Theatre*. Buffalo, NY: D.O.K., 1990.

Kline, Suzy. *The Herbie Jones Readers' Theater: Funny Scenes to Read Aloud*. New York: Putnam, 1992.

Laughlin, M. K., and K. H. Latrobe. *Readers Theatre for Children*. Englewood, CO: Teacher Ideas Press, 1990.

Shepherd, Aaron. *Folktales on Stage: Sixteen Scripts for Readers Theatre from Folk and Fairy Tales of the World*. Bronx, NY: H. W. Wilson, 1993.

Sierra, Judy. 1996. *Multicultural Folktales for Feltboard and Reader's Theatre*. Phoenix, AZ: Oryx Press, 1996.

Books for How and Why (Pourquoi) Stories

Bruchac, Joseph. *Native American Animal Stories*. Golden, CO: Fulcrum Publishing, 1992.

Greaves, Nick. *When Lion Could Fly and Other Tales from Africa*. Hauppauge, NY: Barron's, 1993.

Hamilton, Martha, and Mitch Weiss. *How & Why Stories: World Tales Kids Can Read & Tell*. Little Rock, AR: August House, 1999.

Leach, Maria. *How the People Sang the Mountains Up: How and Why Stories*. New York: Viking Press, 1967.

Scheer, George F. *Cherokee Animal Tales*. Tulsa, OK: Council Oak Books, 1968.

Web Sites for Readers Theatre and Pourquoi Stories

(All Web sites accessed March 1, 2004)

http://www.aaronshep.com—information on using readers theatre, sample scripts, newsletter, and an extensive list of resources.

http://emints.more.net/ethemes/resources/S00001005.html—many Internet links and resources for pourquoi tales and how to write them.

http://www.lisablau.com—lists books available and offers free scripts.

http://www.scriptsforschools.com—description of readers theatre, materials available, and sample scripts.

http://www.storycart.com—information and sample scripts.

http://www.teacherideaspress.com—readers theatre books and scripts.

http://tlc.epsb.ca/aauthor/buchholz/pourquoi.htm—provides several links to prepare students for writing and publishing their own pourquoi tales.

NOTE: Use a search engine to locate other Web sites for readers theatre and pourquoi tales.

Alphabetical Index to Stories

About the Author

Judy Wolfman, a retired elementary school teacher, is now an author, professional storyteller, presenter of workshops, and adjunct professor for two colleges where she teaches storytelling.

As a professional storyteller, Judy has performed throughout the United States, as well as in a few foreign countries and on cruise ships. She is a member of several storytelling groups, including the National Storytelling Network.

A freelance writer, Judy also writes articles and short stories for a variety of adult and children's magazines. She has written three children's plays, several readers theatre scripts, and nine children's nonfiction picture books for the "Life on a Farm" series, published by Carolrhoda Books.

Judy resides in York, PA, with her husband. There she continues to write, tell stories, and present classes and workshops. She has three married children and four granddaughters.

CPSIA information can be obtained at www.ICGtesting.com
Printed in the USA
BVOW05s0514250913

332104BV00001B/81/P